MICKEY MOUSE

WALT DISNEY
MICKEY MOUSE

ABBEVILLE PRESS, INC., PUBLISHERS • NEW YORK, N.Y.

Library of Congress Cataloging In Publication Data

Disney (Walt) Productions.
   Walt Disney best comics—Mickey Mouse.

   (Walt Disney best comic series)
   SUMMARY: Examines the development of the Mickey Mouse comics using the comic strips which have appeared in newspapers and comic books over the years.
   [1. Mickey Mouse (Cartoon character) 2. Cartoons and comics] I. Title. II. Title: Mickey Mouse. III. Series.
PZ6728.M46D585 1978   741.5'973   78-15264
ISBN 0-89659-604-4

THE STORIES

Walt Disney
MICKEY MOUSE

INTRODUCTION

BY FLOYD GOTTFREDSON

Walt Disney was born in Chicago on December 5, 1901, the son of Elias Disney, an Irish-Canadian building contractor, and Flora Call, of German-American descent. Walt had three brothers and one sister: Roy, who joined Walt in business; Raymond, an insurance agent; Herbert, a postman, who died very young; and Ruth, who now lives in Portland, Oregon.

MICKEY MOUSE IS AN ACTOR. And as such he can do anything; he can play any role. At times, he is unassuming, sometimes even shy and naive. But when the situation calls for it, he is resourceful, clever, scrappy, and as brave as any super-hero. He was a bungler in THE SORCERER'S APPRENTICE, according to Dukas' conception of the apprentice. But in THE BRAVE LITTLE TAILOR and the "Happy Valley" sequence of FUN AND FANCY FREE (better known as "Mickey and the Beanstalk"), he was a giant-killer.

I came to know all sides of Mickey well, as I worked with him for nearly forty-six years at The Walt Disney Studio. I joined the Studio in December 1929, as an apprentice animator, or in-betweener. The studio staff was then working on the sixteenth Mickey Mouse short subject, titled JUST MICKEY, and the seventh and eighth of the Silly Symphonies, AUTUMN and CANNIBAL CAPERS.

Mickey Mouse had been conceived on a train carrying Walt and his wife, Lillian, from New York back to Hollywood. Walt, having just lost his successful cartoon character Oswald the Lucky Rabbit to a rival producer in New York, was faced with the task of having to

create a new one. He and Lillian had been reminiscing nostalgically about some pet mice he had tried to train in a small animation studio in Kansas City that he had been running with his artist friend, Ub Iwerks. Walt felt that the new character should be a mouse and came up with the name, Mortimer Mouse. Lillian thought that Mortimer was a little too pretentious and suggested Mickey. So, Mickey Mouse got his name. But Walt still wasn't sure what he would look like.

Back at the studio, after conferences with his artists, Walt and Ub designed Mickey as he appeared in PLANE CRAZY, the first Mickey Mouse animated film produced. In this picture Mickey's eyes were complete ovals with solid black pupils. He wore no gloves or shoes and his hands and feet were black. His pants were short and tight with two buttons in the front, the originals of the slightly looser, two-button short pants which eventually became so famous.

In GALLOPIN' GAUCHO, the second Mickey Mouse film, Mickey had acquired white shoes, but still no gloves. In this picture, Mickey's eyes changed. The ovals around his pupils were eliminated, and his black-spot eyes were drawn directly on the white of his face.

When he was nine years old, Walt Disney delivered newspapers for his father, who had purchased a large newspaper route in Kansas City. In the little spare time he had, he liked to play tennis, but it was the world of the theater which fascinated him most. He and a friend, Walt Pfeiffer, even put together a small vaudeville act, THE TWO WALTS, which enjoyed a moderate local success. But it was only after years of struggle and hard work that Walt finally found his niche in show business and was able to open his first real studio in Hollywood.

By 1929, in THE KARNIVAL KID, Mickey finally had his white gloves, and in medium shots and close-ups he had pie-slice-shaped highlights in his black eyes. This, then, was the basic design which became so well-known all over the world. Because Mickey was an actor, he did change his costume from time to time to fit the role he was playing. But basically his appearance remained unchanged until 1938.

At that time, Walt gave a staff party to celebrate the completion of SNOW WHITE, and Mickey appeared on the cover of the program with white oval eyes the size of his traditional black ones, and with black pupils in them. So, in a way, Mickey's eyes had come full circle (forgive me), though drawn with smaller white ovals than in the original 1929 version.

The first public use of these eyes was in THE SORCERER'S APPRENTICE segment of FANTASIA. FANTASIA, however, was not released until 1940, so the first film actually

Above: Walt Disney with his wife, Lillian Bounds, one of his first valuable collaborators, and their daughter Diane.

Top left: Walt Disney (far right) with his first collaborators, among them, his brother, Roy (fourth from left) and Ub Iwerks (sixth from left).

Bottom left: The whole staff, assembled on the occasion of their first, highly prized Oscar award, received in 1932 for Flowers and Trees. Every year from 1934 to 1940, the Disney Studio won an Oscar.

shown which utilized these new eyes was the Mickey Mouse short, THE POINTER, which was released in 1939. In 1936, Mickey had begun to phase out his traditional short red pants and go more and more to long ones which, except in various merchandising items, he wears to-day.

On January 13, 1930, at the request of King Features Syndicate, Walt launched the daily Mickey Mouse newspaper comic strip. The format of the strip during the first

two and a half months was a different gag every day featuring Mickey, first on a tropical island with islanders and various comic animals, then back in his own neighborhood with Minnie. The first eighteen strips were written by Walt, penciled by Ub Iwerks and inked by Win Smith. In early March, King Features Syndicate, which was distributing the strip, asked Walt to change its story line to a continuous adventure with the humorous Disney touch. This was the trend in comic strips at that

time, following the huge success of THE GUMPS which had that kind of continuity.

So, on March 31, 1930, the first of many such episodes in the daily Mickey Mouse comic strip made its debut. That continuity is the first of those reproduced in this book, under the title, MICKEY MOUSE IN DEATH VALLEY. Walt continued to write the strip until early April, when Win Smith decided to leave the studio. Walt asked me to take the strip over for two weeks until he found someone to do it permanently. Apparently, because of his many other involvements, he forgot to look, and I continued to do it until my retirement in 1975, forty-five and a half years later.

I took over the writing as well as penciling and inking, and the first

1950. Walt Disney and his office with Card Walker, now president of Walt Disney Productions, Harry Tytle, television producer, and Bill Walsh, writer and producer of many films, including Mary Poppins and The Love Bug.

of my work appeared on May 5, 1930 (coincidentally, my birthday)· I wrote the stories until late 1932, when I was assigned a writer. I continued to plot most of the stories, then the writer and I would bat around the following week's continuity and gags until we had them fairly well broken down into panels. Then he would write it up and I would draw it. During the more than forty-five years I drew the strip, I worked with seven different writers, namely: Ted Osborne, Merrill de Maris, Bob Karp, Dick Shaw, Bill Walsh, Roy Williams and Del Connell—all of them good and all of them great to work with.

Our primary thought always was to bring to the strip the spirit and personality of the Mickey Mouse movies. Of course, the comic strip was an entirely different medium. But, knowing that Mickey was basically an actor who could do anything, we felt that the Mickey we were presenting was compatible with the film Mickey, and that we were not developing different personality.

Our approach to the continuities which appeared all through the 30's and 40's and until mid-1955 was to do tongue-in-cheek versions of whatever was currently popular in live-acting Hollywood films or to echo other entertainments which were the fad at that time. And so it was that we were able to have such a wonderfully free-swinging time writing and drawing such strips as are reproduced in this volume.

Haunted houses and westerns were very popular at that time. So, appropriately Walt started the MICKEY MOUSE IN DEATH VALLEY continuity and I carried it on. Pegleg Pete and Sylvester Shyster, both created by Walt, were great villains to work opposite Mickey and Minnie. Pegleg Pete became probably the most perennial heavy of all time, popping up in our stories off and on for twenty years. Pete was especially good to use opposite Mickey because of the great contrast in size and personality.

Carnivals, horse races and steeplechases were big in 1933. Hence, Mickey's funny horse, Tanglefoot, who certainly lived up to his name in our story, MICKEY MOUSE AND HIS HORSE TANGLEFOOT. Especially

popular at that time were who-done-its, the production of numerous movies featuring Sherlock Holmes, Phillip Marlowe, Perry Mason, and others. So we did several spoofs of them through the years the first of which was MICKEY MOUSE THE DETECTIVE. This featured Dippy Dawg, who later evolved into Mickey's mixed up side-kick, Goofy. Actually Dippy Dawg was first introduced in Mickey's films, and incorporated into the strip at Walt's suggestion. This was a fairly common practice; and often when Walt felt that a film creation could become a permanent member of his cast of characters, he would ask us to bring him into the comic strip.

Hollywood films featuring Africa, North Africa, Arabia and the French Foreign Legion were other rages in those days, so we sent Mickey to those exotic places in MICKEY AND THE SACRED JEWEL and MICKEY MOUSE AND THE FOREIGN LEGION. And in both of these, the perennial bad guy, Pegleg Pete, appears again.

Science fiction with benign professors and mad scientists, eerie laboratories and weird machines were in full bloom in the 30's. Two of our versions were MICKEY MOUSE AND THE PIRATE SUBMARINE and MICKEY MOUSE ON SKY ISLAND. Pegleg Pete pops up again in the second of these.

Gangster films, such as *Little Caesar,* were all over the scenes. Mickey dips into this shadowy underworld in MICKEY MOUSE RUNS HIS OWN NEWSPAPER. Peg-

leg Pete, of course, is head gangster. Donald Duck appears for the first time in a newspaper comic strip in this continuity, but his appearance will change quite a bit in the next few years.

MICKEY MOUSE ADVENTURES WITH ROBIN HOOD we did in the

full-color Sunday page instead of the black-and-white daily strip. We felt a version of this classic needed color for best presentation.

MICKEY MOUSE AND THE SEVEN GHOSTS was especially notable for the first comic strip appearance of Goofy as Goofy and not as his

Mickey Mouse shows us how an animated cartoon is produced at Walt Disney Studios. 1. In the Story-Board Department, Chip sketches the main phases of the action on sheets of paper, which are then tacked to the "story board," like drawings in a comic strip. Later, they will be modified, expanded, or reduced to become the sequence of the animated cartoon. 2. Music is created in the Sound Department. It must fit the dialogue and express the setting and the at-

original, Dippy Dawg. Also, this marked Donald Duck's first appearance in close to his present form.

Trying always to reflect in the Mickey Mouse comic strip what was being done in the Mickey Mouse films, we would deliberately bring Mickey home from one of his wild adventures and let him settle down for a week or so, doing homey, gag-a-day strips to re-establish his basic personality.

Through the years Mickey's personality underwent, generally, the same sort of evolution as his appearance did. At first it was quite simple and limited, but it broadened and became more mature and sophisticated as the creative personnel of the Studio grew. Of course, being an actor, his personality broadened and became more active when he was involved in the more adventurous and sophisticated film vehicles. But always, behind it all, was his basically warm, charming self with a universal appeal which everyone, including Walt, had difficulty defining. I think the best definition I ever heard was Walt's own, when he said in an early interview:

mosphere. 3. In the Layout and Background Department, skilled artists sketch in backgrounds. Like the soundtrack, the visual background must support and strengthen the action. 4. In the Animation Department, the animator must catch the right expression and the right movement to convey the spirit of the drawings into motion. 5. In the Ink and Paint Department, the pencil drawings made in the Animation Department are recopied by a duplicating process onto sheets of transparent celluloid. Each "cel" is hand painted, like figures in a coloring book. 6. The story is brought to

Sometimes I've tried to figure out why Mickey appealed to the whole world. Everybody's tried to figure it out. So far as I know, nobody has. He's a pretty nice fellow who never does anybody any harm, who gets into scrapes through no fault of his own, but aways manages to come up grinning. Why Mickey's even been faithful to one girl, Minnie, all his life. Mickey is so simple and uncomplicated, so easy to understand, that you can't help liking him.

Mickey was my very exciting and satisfying companion for nearly forty-six years. And he is still very much alive and well. He is the official host for both Disneyland and Walt Disney World. He is the welcoming host for the Mickey Mouse Club television series, both old and new. And he appears on merchandising items such as toys, clothing, books, and many others. In newspaper daily comic strips and Sunday pages he is the Walt Disney symbol and a good-will ambassador all over the world, where he is instantly recognized and welcomed by everyone. Long may he reign!

the screen in the Camera Department. Normally, the "cels" are placed one above the other against the backgrounds and photographed for individual frames of the movie. 7. When the boss makes sure that sound track—voices, orchestration, sound effects—synchronizes perfectly with the images, he gives the go-ahead to print copies of the final film. 8. Though we know the story and have worked on the movie, we, too, are eager to sit back in our Projection Room and watch the movie unfold. This is the happiest and most exciting moment.

MICKEY'S GUIDE TO FAMILIAR
WALT DISNEY COMIC CHARACTERS

In the beginning—I mean, in 1930—my daily comic strips were created and published only in black-and-white, although the halftone screen made it possible to achieve effective and suggestive contrasts between light and shadow. In January of 1932, Walt Disney Enterprises began the production of Sunday comic strips in color. That first story was titled MICKEY MOUSE AND THE DOGCATCHER. Almost simultaneously, the public was presented with Disney's first color film, the short subject FLOWER AND TREES.

Disney characters have come and gone, but they remain fresh in our memories, as clear and specific representatives of their era. Each one is linked to the period and setting in which it was created. I'd like to introduce a few of them."

KAT NIPP　　　**MR. SLICKER**　　　**SYLVESTER SHYSTER**　　　**UNCLE MORTIMER**

RUFFHOUSE RAT　　　**CREAMO CATNERA**　　　**BUCKY BUG**　　　**MAYOR BUGG**

16

| 1932 | 1932 | 1933 | 1933 |

PROF. ECKS & DOUBLEX   **CAPT. CHURCHMOUSE**   **MORTIMER MOUSE**   **TANGLEFOOT**

| 1933 | 1933 | 1934 | 1935 |

MR. GLOOMY   **CAPTAIN DOBERMAN**   **DON JOLLIO**   **MR. SQUINCH**

| 1935 | 1935 | 1935 | 1935 |

MAX HARE   **TOBY TORTOISE**   **ELMER**   **INKY, CALICO, FLUFF**

1935

DR. VULTER

1936

OSCAR

1936

TRIGGER HAWKES

1936

THE BIG BAD WOLF

1936

DOCTOR EINMUG

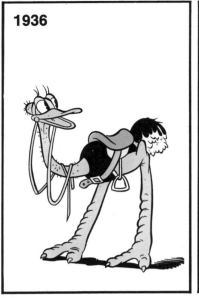

1937

LITTLE HIAWATHA

1939

JOE PIPER

1939

MR. CASEY

1939

THE "BLOT"

1939

MR. O'HARA

1947

PFLIP

1947

EEGA BEEVA

GRAPHIC DEVELOPMENT
1930-1970

On January 13, 1930, certain newspapers in the United States published the first comic strip of my adventures. But, as you know, I had already been known since 1928 when my first, famous animated cartoon, STEAMBOAT WILLIE, was shown. Since then my friends and I have traveled a long road, and we have undergone inevitable changes: little by little we have adjusted ourselves to the time. The technical requirements of animated cartoons also required certain added touches or substitutions; my

artists always pursued new sources of inspiration, and while their drawing kept gaining incisiveness and maturity, achieving greater and unquestionable artistic value, the times and the events of history followed each other at a dizzying pace.

A direct and immediate comparison between the old and the new may prove curious and interesting. For that reason, I thought you would like to see the graphic development of some of the principal characters of the Disney stories.

MICKEY MOUSE

MINNIE MOUSE

HORACE HORSECOLLAR

CLARABELLE COW

PEGLEG PETE

1931

1938

PLUTO

1932

1936

1968

DIPPY DAWG, LATER GOOFY

1934

1935

1969

DONALD DUCK

EXPRESSIONS AND IMAGES

The power of expression, the outer display of inner emotions, is marked by the lines, furrows, and tensions of certain muscles or certain nerves in the human face.

Cartoonists who humanize the physiognomies of animals create a great challenge for themselves in attempting to mimic human expressions with animal forms.

In characters created by Walt Disney, we find practically all the human anatomical elements, all the simple and characteristic expressive lines, which an artist will use to draw people.

On these two pages, I will show you a few expressions or gestures so you can see how the anatomy of cartoon characters allows for a wide range of expression.

EXHAUSTION   EXASPERATION   SATISFACTION   DESOLATION

DELIBERATION   SHREWDNESS   SADNESS

SURPRISE   SHOCK   WHISPERING   PLEADING

FEAR

WORRY

SHOUTING

JOY

GREED

FRUSTRATION

SLEEPINESS

WONDER

ACCUSATION

COMMAND

REBELLION

WALT DISNEY AROUND THE WORLD

The strength of the Disney language—that is, the powerful vein of subtle humor that runs through his characters, the immediacy and warmth of their communication, their delightfully human personalities—has been transformed into a universal language and today his characters are known, esteemed, and admired all over the world. They are present in twenty-four nations and speak seventeen different languages. Here, are the names of some of Walt's chief characters in nine languages.

ENGLISH

MICKEY MOUSE
MINNIE MOUSE
GOOFY
JIMINY CRICKET
DONALD DUCK
PLUTO
DAISY DUCK
GRANDMA DUCK
BIG PETE
BEAGLE BOYS
UNCLE SCROOGE
GYRO GEARLOOSE
BIG BAD WOLF
CHIP & DALE
GLADSTONE
DEWEY
HUEY
LOUIE

ITALIAN

TOPOLINO
MINNI
PIPPO
GRILLO SAGGIO
PAPERINO
PLUTO
PAPERINA
NONNA PAPERA
GAMBADILEGNO
BASSOTTI
ZIO PAPERONE
ARCHIMEDE PITAGORICO
LUPO EZECHIELE
CIP e CIOP
GASTONE
QUI
QUO
QUA

ENGLISH

MICKEY MOUSE
MINNIE MOUSE
GOOFY
JIMINY CRICKET
DONALD DUCK
PLUTO
DAISY DUCK
GRANDMA DUCK
BIG PETE
BEAGLE BOYS
UNCLE SCROOGE
GYRO GEARLOOSE
BIG BAD WOLF
CHIP & DALE
GLADSTONE
DEWEY
HUEY
LOUIE

YUGLOSLAV

MIKI MAUS
MINI MAUS
SILJA
CVRCA CVRCAK
PAJA PATAK
PLUTON
PATA
BAKA PATA
VELIKI PIT
BULDOZI
CIKA BAJA
PROKA PRONALAZAC
ZAO VUK
CIP I DEJL
SRETSKO SRETSKOVITS
GAIO
RAIO
VLAIO

FRENCH

MICKEY
MINNIE
DINGO
JIMINY
DONALD
PLUTO
DAISY
GRAND'MERE CANE
PAT HIBULAIRE
LES RAPETOUT
ONCLE PICSOU
GEO TROUVETOUT
LE GRAND MECHANT LOUP
TIC & TAC
GONTRAN BONHEUR
FIFI
RIRI
LOULOU

GERMAN

MICKEY MAUS
MINNIE MAUS
GOOFY
JIMINY GRILLE
DONALD DUCK
PLUTO
DAISY DUCK
OMA DUCK
KATER KARLO
PANZERKNACKER
ONKEL DAGOBERT
DANIEL DÜSENTRIEB
DER GROSSE BÖSE WOLF
A- UND BEHÖRNCHEN
GUSTAV GANS
TRICK
TICK
TRACK

NORWEGIAN

MIKKE MUS
MINNI MUS
LANGBEIN
TIMMI GRESSHOPPE
DONALD DUCK
PLUTO
DOLLY DUCK
BESTEMOR DUCK
SVARTE-PETTER
B-GJENGEN
ONKEL SKRUE
PETTER SMART
DEN STORE STYGGE ULVEN
SNIPP OG SNAPP
HELDIGE ANTON
DOLE
OLE
DOFFEN

GREEK

ΜΙΚΥ ΜΑΟΥΣ
ΜΙΝΙ ΜΑΟΥΣ
ΓΚΟΥΦΗ
ΓΡΥΛΟΣ
ΝΤΟΝΑΛΝΤ ΝΤΑΚ
ΠΛΟΥΤΟ
ΝΤΑΙΖΗ ΝΤΑΚ
ΓΙΑΓΙΑ ΝΤΑΚ
ΜΑΥΡΟΣ ΠΗΤ
ΣΥΜΜΟΡΙΑ ΛΥΚΩΝ
ΘΕΙΟΣ ΣΚΡΟΥΤΖ
ΚΥΡΟΣ
ΚΑΚΟΣ ΛΥΚΟΣ
ΤΣΙΠ ΚΑΙ ΝΤΑΙΗΛ
ΓΚΑΣΤΟΝΕ
ΝΤΙΟΥΗ
ΧΙΟΥΗ
ΛΙΟΥΗ

JAPANESE

ミッキー （マウス）
ミニー （マウス）
グーフィー
ジミニー クリケット
ドナルド （ダック）
プルート
デージー （ダック）

スクルージ おじさん

わる おおかみ
チップ と デール

デューイ
ヒューイ
ルイ

ARABIC

ميكى
ميى
بندى

دونالد
بلوتو
ديزى
الجدة كينه
بطرس
عصابة القناع الاسود
عم دهب
عبقرينو
الثعلب المكار

محظوظ
لولو
سوسو
توتو

MICKEY MOUSE IN DEATH VALLEY

MICKEY MOUSE IN DEATH VALLEY

31

OH, MICKEY'S BEEN GONE SUCH A LONG TIME. I'M SO SORRY I BAWLED HIM OUT! I WISH HE'D COME BACK SOON!

HEY!

EEK!!

IT'S ME, MINNIE! HOW'S THIS SCARECROW FOR SHELTER?

MICKEY!!

WE'RE SINGING IN THE RAIN!

IN THE MORNING--

I'LL BRING MINNIE SOME MILK FROM THIS COW!

MOOOO!

MOOO!

YOU RUNT! I HOPE ALL YOUR CALVES GROW UP AND GIVE SOUR MILK!

LOOK, MINNIE! I REALLY USE MY HEAD!

SEE? I'LL LEAVE THE LINES IN THE WATER FOR A WHILE AND EACH ONE WILL COME UP WITH A FISH!

OKAY, MINNIE! GET READY TO CATCH THE FISH!

WHEN THIS IS ROASTED, I'LL GIVE YOU THE PART WITH THE WISH-BONE!

GOOD! I'LL WISH WE BEAT OLD SHYSTER TO DEATH VALLEY!

I WONDER WHAT HAPPENED TO OUR OLD FRIEND THE FOX?

WE COULD SURE USE HIS HELP NOW?

OH, MICKEY! SHYSTER AND PEG-LEG MUST BE MILES AND MILES AHEAD OF US-- MAYBE WE OUGHT TO GIVE UP AND TURN BACK!

NEVER! I'M A ONE-WAY GUY AND THAT'S FORWARD!

HEY! WHAT'S THAT NOISE?

IT'S COMING FROM OVER THE HILL! IT SOUNDS LIKE A CAR!

BANG!

HURRY, MINNIE! MAYBE THEY'LL GIVE US A LIFT TO DEATH VALLEY!

LOOK! IT'S SHYSTER AND PEG-LEG!

THEY MUST HAVE BEEN OVER THE HILL THIS WHOLE TIME!

DARN THIS CAR, BOSS! I CAN'T SEEM TO FIX.

YOU'VE BEEN TRYING FOR A WEEK, YOU BONEHEAD! YOU MUST HAVE A BRAND-NEW BRAIN-- YOU'VE NEVER USED IT!

SO! I'VE CAUGHT YOU AT LAST! HAND OVER THAT MAP.

DO YOU UNDERSTAND?-- GIVE ME THE MAP RIGHT NOW!

WHY, I NEVER SAW THESE RUNTS BEFORE IN MY LIFE!

I NEVER SAW THEM EITHER! NOW GET OUT OF HERE!

BUT MICKEY DOES NOT GIVE UP SO EASILY...

RUN, MINNIE! I HAVE AN IDEA!

PULL HARD, MINNIE! AS A BRAKEMAN, HE'S ALL WET!

GOOD IDEA, HUH?

SO MICKEY AND MINNIE GET AWAY, AND FINALLY THEY NEAR THEIR GOAL...

WELCOME TO POISON WELLS, GATEWAY TO DEATH VALLEY!
LOOK! WE'RE ALMOST THERE!

TIENDA GENERAL NO CREDITO
BALOON
THIS IS JUST LIKE A MOVIE. I FEEL THE CALL OF THE WEST ALREADY!

COME ON, MINNIE, WE'LL GET A JOB IN THIS TOWN SO WE CAN BUY OUTFITS FOR OUR TRIP INTO THE DESERT!

WANTED WAITRESS AND DISHWASHER
HERE'S THE JOBS FOR US!

FRENCHY, WE'LL TAKE THE JOBS!
OUI? CAN YOU WASH ZEE DEESHES GOOD?

WELL, I HIRE ZEE BOTH OF YOU — YOU START ZEE WORK RIGHT NOW!
HURRAY!

TIME FLIES... FOUR MORE DAYS OF WORK AND WE CAN BUY THOSE OUTFITS!

MEANWHILE... YOUR FEET COULDN'T HURT AS MINE DO — YOU ONLY HAVE HALF AS MANY!

AH, PETE! YOU'RE FINALLY BECOMING USEFUL!

ONLY TWO MORE DAYS TO GO, MINNIE!
WAITER!

POISON WELLS, HUH?! I HOPE THE FOOD DOESN'T LIVE UP TO THE NAME!
HEY, WAITER! LET'S HAVE SOME SERVICE HERE!

EEK! IT'S SHYSTER AND PEGLEG!
WHAT??

WHAT ARE WE GOING TO DO? WE CAN'T LET THEM FIND US!

SERVICE! I WANT SERVICE NOW!
DO SOMETHING, MICKEY!
I HAVE AN IDEA! I'LL MAKE A DISGUISE AND THEY WON'T KNOW ME!

AH! FINALLY! BRING US A COUPLE OF STEAKS, QUICK!

SAY, OLD TIMER, DID YOU EVER HEAR OF A DESERTED GOLD MINE CALLED THE MORTIMER MINE?
NOPE! I AIN'T NEVER HEARD OF NO MUCH MINE!

DARN THIS PEPPER. I CAN HARDLY GET ANYTHING OUT OF IT!

THERE! THAT'S MORE LIKE IT!
A-A-A-

·AH-CHOO!

IT'S MICKEY!

AND THE CHASE IS ON...

KITCHEN
RUN, MINNIE! AS FAST AS YOU CAN!

YOU DUMBHEAD! YOU'RE BLOCKING MY WAY!
BUT MY LEG IS STUCK!

LOOK! JUST WHAT WE NEED FOR OUR EXPEDITION!
GUNS
SOMBREROS
SUPPLIES
BOOTS · SADDLES

THIS HAT SHOULD PROTECT ME FROM THE DESERT SUN!

WELL, MINNIE! DO I LOOK LIKE A COWBOY?

OH YES, MICKEY! HOW ABOUT ME?

BUT LOOK WHO'S HERE...

OH MY GOSH, MINNIE! IT'S SHYSTER AND PETE!

STAND ON MY SHOULDERS, MINNIE, AND DON'T LOSE YOUR BALANCE!

SAY, HAVE YOU SEEN TWO LITTLE RUNTS AROUND HERE?

NOPE!

OUTFITS FOR DESERT TRIPS

BOOTS FOR SALE

C'MON, HORSIE, LET'S GO— GIDDAP!

GIPDAP!

STUPID CACTUS, YOU RUINED EVERYTHING!

?

LET'S GET OUT OF HERE, MINNIE! HANG ON TIGHT!

YOU BRAINLESS NUMBSKULL YOU LET THEM ESCAPE!

LET'S GRAB THOSE TWO HORSES AND CATCH UP WITH THEM!

BUT...

HEY!

HORSE THIEVES! AFTER 'EM, MEN!

?? ???

SALOON

GO GET 'EM, SHERIFF!

CATCH THEM THIEVES!

YOU CROOK! TRY THIS OLD WESTERN CUSTOM AROUND YOUR NECK!

BANG!

LYNCH 'EM DIRTY THIEVES!

HELP, BOSS!

STICK 'EM UP, HOMBRE!

COME ON, LET'S HANG THE VARMINTS!

I DEMAND A JURY TRIAL— I'LL SWEAR OUT A HABEAS CORPUS!

WE'RE THE JURY AND THE VERDICT IS GUILTY!

TO THE OLD OAK TREE!

IT'S BACK TO THE TREES FOR YOU GORILLAS!

HEY, THEY CAN'T HANG ME FOR A HORSE THIEF— I TOOK A MULE!

GEE, MICKEY, WE FINALLY GOT AWAY FROM OLD SHYSTER, WE'VE GOT THE MAP, PLENTY OF PROVISIONS! THE FUTURE LOOKS VERY BRIGHT!

YOU SAID IT, MINNIE!

WE'RE REAL GOLD-HUNTERS NOW, MINNIE— I'LL PRETEND I'M AN OLD DESERT PROSPECTOR DOMINATED BY THE DESIRE FOR GOLD— GOLD-GOLD!

♪ LOO-KIN' AT THE WORLD THROUGH ROSE-COLORED GLASSES ♪

...THERE THEY WERE—ONE HUNDRED INDIANS WAVING THEIR TOMAHAWKS, YELLING FOR MY SCALP—I KNEW IF I LOST MY HEAD THEY'D HAVE MY SCALP—BUT I WASN'T AFRAID—I HAD TO THINK FAST—AND I DID...

I GRITTED MY TEETH AND CHARGED TOWARD THEM AND CAPTURED THEM ALL—**ONE HUNDRED INDIANS!**

YOU CAPTURED THEM ALL **SINGLE-HANDED?** HOW?

I SURROUNDED THEM!

OOH GEE!

?

IN THE MORNING, MICKEY, MINNIE, AND THEIR FRIEND THE OLD DESERT RAT CONTINUE ON THEIR WAY TO THE GOLD MINE!

THIS HERE DESERT WAS ONCE COLDER'N THE SOUTH POLE—NOW TAKE THAT THERE NATCHERAL BRIDGE—ACCORDIN' TO THE INDIANS—IT'S A RAINBOW THAT FROZE SO SOLID THAT IT'S NEVER THAWED OUT SINCE!

THE SAME WINTER A BIG ELEPHANT FROZE—THAR'S HIS FEET STILL A' STANDIN'!

GUESS YOU WONDER WHY I DON'T TAKE SOME GOLD FROM YOUR UNCLE'S MINE AND GO PLACES—WELL, THE DESERT'S GOOD ENOUGH FOR ME!

AH HA! AT LAST WE'RE ON THE RIGHT TRAIL. HERE'S THEIR TRACKS!

THEY MUSTA BEEN JOINED BY SOMEONE AT THIS ADOBE SHACK—THERE'S 3 OF 'EM NOW AND ANOTHER MULE!

THEY CAMPED HERE LAST NIGHT! THESE ASHES ARE STILL WARM!

AND HERE'S A BOX OF MICKEY'S FAVORITE CHEESE!

COME ON, MEN! WE CAN'T BE MORE THAN A FEW HOURS BEHIND THEM—WE'LL CATCH MICKEY AND LYNCH HIM ON SIGHT!

WE'LL COME UP TO THE CRYIN' JOSHUA TREES TOMORROW—I CAN HEAR FAINT WEEPIN' NOW—

STOP! QUIET, MEN! I SMELL SMOKE!

GUESS YOU CAN'T HEAR 'EM 'CAUSE YOU AIN'T USED TO THE DESERT—BUT YOU'LL HEAR 'EM TOMORROW!

THERE THEY ARE—WE'VE GOT 'EM!

OKAY, WE'LL SURROUND 'EM. HIDE BEHIND THOSE ROCKS TILL I GIVE THE SIGNAL!

GET 'EM, MEN!

AND ...

WHAT ?!?

STICK 'EM UP! AND DON'T MAKE A FALSE MOVE!

BANG!

THIS MUST BE THE MAP HE STOLE FROM YOU, SHYSTER!

KEEP 'EM UP THERE!

YOU'RE PLUMB LOCO, SHERIFF—THE MAP IS MINNIE'S!

BE QUIET, MOUSE—IT'S THE END OF THE ROPE FOR YOU! RIGHT NOW!

THIS IS THE MAP, ALL RIGHT!

YOU CAN'T LYNCH MICKEY! WHAT IF HE'S INNOCENT?

THEN WE'LL APOLOGIZE TO MINNIE!

HERE'S A GOOD TREE OVER HERE, SHERIFF!

45

THERE HE IS! FIND A LOW PLACE ON THE BANKS TO CATCH HIM!

I'LL HAVE TO GET TO THE OTHER SIDE OF THE RIVER TO ESCAPE FROM THE POSSE!

I WISH I HAD SOMETHING TO STEER WITH! IF THEY FIND A BREAK IN THAT HIGH BANK, I'M LOST!

I'VE CAUGHT BANDITS, COLDS AN' THE 5:15! BUT I MAY AS WELL BE CHASING RAINBOWS AS CATCHING THIS MICKEY MOUSE!

HEY, I FOUND A BRANCH TO STEER WITH!

GEE, I SURE HOPE MINNIE IS OKAY! DURN OLD SHYSTER FOR MAKING A FUGITIVE OF ME!

LOOKIT THOSE GUYS! HOW WILL I EVER LOSE THEM?!

IT'S NO USE, SHERIFF—WE MIGHT HAVE TO RIDE FOR DAYS BEFORE GETTIN' DOWN TO THE RIVER!

YER RIGHT, HANK! WE'RE JEST WASTIN' TIME— WE'LL TURN THIS CHASE OVER TO THE RANGERS WHO KNOW THIS COUNTRY!

COME ON! WE'LL GO BACK AND JAIL THAT OLD DESERT RAT AND MINNIE AS ACCOMPLICES!

GOSH! I HAVEN'T SEEN THE POSSE! I WONDER WHERE THEY ARE?

COME ON, "PUG"—PACK UP! WE'RE TAKIN' THESE TWO TO JAIL UNTIL THAT LITTLE OUTLAW IS CAUGHT!

OH, GOODY! THEY DIDN'T CATCH HIM!

YOU COME WITH ME! YOU'LL TELL ME WHERE MICKEY'S HIDEOUT IS, OR ELSE!

I'LL FIND MICKEY WITH YOUR HELP!

HOLY MACKERAL! THIS RIVER'S GETTIN' ROUGHER AND SWIFTER BY THE MINUTE!

THIS IS TERRIBLE! I CAN'T STOP! THE WATER'S JUST RUSHIN' ME ALONG!

WHAT IS THAT NOISE?

AN AWFUL SURPRISE AWAITS MICKEY...

OH NO! THE FALLS!

HELP! OH HELP!

IT'S ALL OVER! I CAN'T LOOK!

50

MICKEY MOUSE AND HIS HORSE TANGLEFOOT

MICKEY MOUSE AND HIS HORSE TANGLEFOOT

56

MICKEY, WHAT MAKES YOU SO SURE TANGLEFOOT WILL WIN?

IT'S A SECRET, BUT I'LL LET YOU IN ON IT!

TANGLEFOOT'S SCARED T' DEATH OF HORNETS— SO ALL I GOTTA DO IS MAKE A NOISE LIKE ONE... BZZZZZZT...

!

...BZZZZZT— AND TANGLEFOOT GOES LIKE A STREAK OF GREASED LIGHTNING! SO YOU SEE WE CAN'T LOSE!

SO THAT'S HOW HE DOES IT, EH?!

HE'S SMART, ALL RIGHT! BUT I'M SMARTER! OH BOY, WHAT AN IDEA I'VE GOT!

9-7 WALT DISNEY

MINNIE, WHERE'D YOU GET ALL THAT MONEY?

I MORTGAGED MY HOUSE, MY FURNITURE, EVERYTHING! I'M GOING TO BET IT ALL ON TANGLEFOOT!

THAT'S SWELL, MINNIE! 'CAUSE I KNOW WE CAN'T LOSE!

POOR MINNIE AND MICKEY! THEY DON'T KNOW WHAT THE GAMBLERS HAVE IN STORE! AND THAT NIGHT...

IF THE HORSE CAN'T HEAR MICKEY'S BZZZZZT, HE WON'T GET SCARED! IF HE DON'T GET SCARED HE WON'T RUN! GET IT?

ALL RIGHT! I'LL HOLD HIS HEAD AND YOU STUFF THE COTTON IN HIS EARS!

9-8

WALT DISNEY

THE NEXT MORNING...

WELL, TANGLEFOOT, HOW'RE YOU FEELIN' TODAY?

THAT'S FUNNY! HE DOESN'T SEEM TO HEAR! HEY TANGLEFOOT!

HEY, TANGLEFOOT!

MINNIE!! MY GOSH! HE'S GONE DEAF!

OH, NO! AND ALL THEIR HOPES ARE PINNED ON TANGLEFOOT!

OH, MICKEY! I'LL LOSE MY HOME!

AND SO WILL I!

AW, GEE, MINNIE! DON'T CRY!

I CAN'T HELP IT! THEY'LL TAKE YOU TO JAIL!

AND POOR TANGLEFOOT WILL GO TO THE GLUE FACTORY! BOO-HOO-HOOOO!

HAVE COURAGE, MINNIE! I'M NO QUITTER! AND THAT RACE AIN'T LOST TILL IT'S OVER!

WALT DISNEY

BUT STILL...THE NIGHT BEFORE THE RACE MICKEY AND TANGLEFOOT ARE BOTH SO NERVOUS THEY CAN'T SLEEP!

DEBTS!

MY HOUSE!

GLUE FACTORY!

MINNIE!

JAIL!

CREDITORS!

OH GOSH!

LISTEN, TANGLEFOOT, WE BOTH GOTTA GET SOME REST!

HALF AN HOUR LATER

Z-Z-Z-Z-Z-Z-Z

Z-Z-Z-Z-Z-Z-Z

THE BUGLES HAVE BLOWN! THE BIG RACE IS ABOUT TO START!

GOODBYE, MICKEY! AND GOOD LUCK!

THANKS, MINNIE!!

SMACK!

GOSH! WITH THAT FOR A STARTER, I CAN'T LOSE!

WHAT THA'?

WALT DISNEY

59

ALL THE HORSES ARE AT THE BARRIER... EXCEPT TANGLE-FOOT... MICKEY IS WORKING FEVERISHLY TO REPAIR THE BROKEN SULKY!

DOGGONE IT! OF ALL THE ROTTEN LUCK!

WHAT'S THE MATTER? THEY CAN'T HOLD UP THE RACE ALL DAY!

I'M COMING! WAIT!

AT LAST! SHE'S ALL FIXED!

GOOD GOSH! THEY STARTED THE RACE WITHOUT ME!

THEY'RE OFF!

POOR TANGLE-FOOT WAS NOT ONLY LEFT AT THE POST — HE WAS LEFT IN THE PADDOCK!

COME ON! LET'S GET GOIN'! AFTER 'EM BOY! AFTER 'EM!

GOOD GRIEF! IT'S THAT MICKEY! HE'S IN A SULKY!

JUDGES

HEY YOU! THIS ISN'T A SULKY RACE! IT'S A STEEPLECHASE! YOU IDIOT!

JUDGES

MICKEY HAS NO CHOICE BUT TO GO ON! HIS WHOLE FUTURE DEPENDS ON THE RESULT OF THIS RACE!

OH GOSH! I'M TOO SCARED TO LOOK!

FIRST BARRIER

HELP!

BAM!

WHOOPEE! YOU MADE IT, TANGLEFOOT!

THE CROWD IS GOING WILD!

KEEP IT UP, TANGLEFOOT! I'M OKAY!

NOW CATCH THOSE OTHER HORSES!

I CAN CUT LOOSE THE HARNESS AND SHAFTS— I WON'T NEED THEM ANY-MORE!

NOW WE'RE ALL SET! AFTER 'EM, OLD FELLOW!

BULLETIN: THE HORSES ARE BUNCHED AT THE FIFTH BARRIER— ALL EXCEPT TANGLEFOOT, WHO IS STILL BETWEEN THE FIRST AND SECOND!

WE GOTTA REALLY GO FAST TO CATCH UP NOW!

TANGLEFOOT! HORNETS!!! BZZZZZT BZZZZT

WHY CAN'T HE HEAR ME?!

MICKEY KEEPS HOPING TANGLE-FOOT WILL REGAIN HIS HEARING! POOR MICKEY!

HA! HA! WE REALLY PUT ONE OVER ON THAT MICK-EY MOUSE!

WE SURE DID, BOSS! HE HASN'T A CHANCE!

IT LOOKS LIKE HE'S TRYIN' TO LOSE! DOES HE WANT TO GO TO JAIL?

TANGLE-FOOT IS ONLY 300 YARDS BEHIND AS HE APPROACH-ES THE SECOND BARRIER!

OKAY TANGLEFOOT! NOW JUMP!

HOORAY!! WE MADE IT!

60

MICKEY MOUSE THE DETECTIVE

MICKEY MOUSE THE DETECTIVE

HELLO, DIPPY! CLARABELLE SAID SHE'LL LEND US SOME FURNITURE. YOU GO DOWN TO HER GARAGE AND PICK OUT WHAT WE NEED!

SWELL! I'LL GO BORROW A TRUCK!

GOOD OL' CLARABELLE! WE'LL HAVE THE BEST OFFICE IN TOWN!

I HOPE DIPPY GOT THE FURNITURE! IT'LL SURE SEEM GOOD TO HAVE AN OFFICE THAT'S DIGNIFIED-LIKE!

DETECTIVE AGENCY
DIPPY DAWG
MICKEY MOUSE
SLEUTHING DONE DIR CHEAP

GENTLEMEN, AS MAYOR OF THIS CITY, I CONGRATULATE YOU ON YOUR NEW DETECTIVE BUSINESS!

GEE! THANKS, MAYOR SCOTT!

BUT OUR FAIR CITY IS TOO HONEST! WHY, THERE HASN'T BEEN A CRIME HERE IN FIVE YEARS!

PARDON ME! THE PHONE...

BRRRRING! RING!

HELLO! WHAT!!!?

GOOD GOSH! MY CAR HAS BEEN STOLEN!

MICKEY AND DIPPY RUSH OUT TO RECOVER MAYOR SCOTT'S STOLEN CAR!

HONK! BEEP! BEEP!

BY GARSH! I'M GONNA COVER THIS TOWN LIKE A WET BLANKET!

WHAM!

DIPPY! THAT WAS THE MAYOR'S CAR! DID YOU SEE WHO WAS DRIVIN'?

NO, BUT DON'T WORRY! WE'LL CATCH HIM!

I GOT HIS LICENSE NUMBER!

RIDING ON TANGLEFOOT, MICKEY AND DIPPY ARE HOT ON THE TRAIL OF THE THIEF!

LOOK! THERE IT IS, DIPPY! IT'S GOT A FLAT TIRE OR SOMETHIN'!

SHHHHHH! WE GOT HIM RED-HANDED!

WE GOT HIM!

HUR-RAY!

SWELL WORK, DIPPY! THIS JOB'LL MAKE US FAMOUS!

HERE YOU ARE, MAYOR SCOTT! WE FOUND YOUR CAR AND THE GUY WHO SWIPED IT!

GREAT! MIGHTY FAST WORK! DID HE PUT UP MUCH OF A FIGHT?

NOT AFTER I SLAMMED HIM A COUPLE IN THE JAW!

WE HAD T' TREAT HIM A LITTLE ROUGH, ON ACCOUNT OF HE WAS TERRIBLE STRONG! HE...

GOOD HEAVENS! MY WIFE!

MICKEY IS IN BAD TROUBLE WITH THE MAYOR—SO HE TRIES TO REDEEM HIMSELF!

BOY, IS HE SORE! MAYBE IF I BRING HIS CAR BACK, HE'LL GET OVER IT!

THERE'S HIS HOUSE AT TH' BOTTOM OF TH' HILL! HEY, THAT'S FUNNY! WHAT'S TH' MATTER WITH THESE BRAKES!?

OH NO!! I CAN'T STOP!

HEY! I THINK YOU BETTER HAVE YOUR BRAKES FIXED! THEY'RE TERRIBLE!

69

GOOD MORNING, MR. BARK! ANYTHING NEW ON THE CASE!?

NUTHIN'— WITH ME AND HOWELL IN TOWN, THEY KNOW THEY HAVEN'T A CHANCE!

GEE! YOU'RE A SWELL DETECTIVE!

YEAH! WHEN WE GET ON A CASE, WE DON'T FOOL WITH 'EM! WE GET 'EM!

ONLY WE'RE USED TO BIG CASES! DINKY ONES LIKE THIS ARE TOO EASY! I'M HARDLY INTERESTED!

OH YA AIN'T? SOME BLINKIN' LOW-LIFE LIFTED FOUR PAIRS OF RED UNDERWEAR FROM MY ROOM LAST NIGHT!

GOOD GOSH, HOWELL!

© 1933, by Walt Disney Enterprises, Great Britain rights reserved.

THE HAIR ROBBERS EVEN GOT YOU!

YEP! I WOKE UP THIS MORNING AND THEY WAS GONE!

© 1933, by Walt Disney Enterprises, Great Britain rights reserved.

BUT WHEN ROBBERS FOOL AROUND WITH A DETECTIVE LIKE ME, THEY BETTER MAKE NO SLIPS!

DID YOU GET A CLUE?

THE BEST CLUE IN THE WORLD! HE LEFT HIS FINGER-PRINTS ON THE WINDOW SILL!

HOT DOG! THE FIRST CLUE! NOW WE'RE GETTIN' SOMEWHERE!

YEP! GREATEST CLUE IN THE WORLD!

BARKE & HOWELL SUPER DETECTIVES

© 1933, by Walt Disney Enterprises, Great Britain rights reserved.

GREAT THING, FINGER-PRINTS! NO TWO PEOPLE HAS GOT THE SAME ONES! HERE— I'LL SHOW YA!

SEE? HERE'S MINE, NEXT TO TH' ROBBER'S!

BUT THEY LOOK JUST ALIKE!

WELL, I'LL BE! I MUSTA TAKEN MY OWN FINGER-PRINTS OFF TH' WINDOW SILL!

HOW'S THE CASE COMIN', MICKEY?

AW, NOT SO GOOD! THOSE DETECTIVES DON'T KNOW MUCH MORE THAN WE DO! ALL THEY'VE FOUND SO FAR IS THEIR OWN FINGER-PRINTS

© 1933, by Walt Disney Enterprises, Great Britain rights reserved.

BUT IT'S A TOUGH CASE! WHO'D WANT MORE RED FLANNELS ANY-WAY? EVERYBODY IN TOWN'S GOT A PAIR!

SOME OF 'EM'S EVEN GOT TWO PAIRS!

LET'S DO SOME DEDUCTIN'! A ROB-BER WOULD TAKE WHAT HE WANTS MOST, HUH?

YUP!

SO WE GOTTA FIGURE WHY HE WANTS RED FLANNELS AN' HAIR MORE 'N MONEY!

IF WE KNEW THE REASON, WE'D HAVE THE CASE SOLVED!

SURE! BUT IT'S EASIER T' SAY IT THAN T' DO IT!

THE NEXT DAY

HERE'S YOUR FIRST WEEK'S SALARY, MICKEY!

GEE, THANKS!

I WANNA DEPOSIT THIS IN TH' SAVINGS BANK!

HMMM! SAY MICKEY, WHERE'D YOU GET THIS MONEY ANY-WAY?

I EARNED IT, OF COURSE! DO YA THINK I SWIPED IT?

OH NO! THAT'S NOT IT AT ALL!

BUT YOU SEE...THIS MONEY IS COUNTERFEIT!

© 1933, by Walt Disney Enterprises, Great Britain rights reserved.

HEY! YOU GUYS PAID ME WITH COUNTERFEIT MONEY!

WHAT??

YEAH! TH' BANK SAID IT WASN'T ANY GOOD AN' THEY KEPT IT!

HURRAY! WHOOPEE!

WHADDAYA MEAN, WHOOPEE?

IT'S WONDERFUL NEWS!

NOW WE GOT A REAL CASE! TO HECK WITH THEM DUMB HAIR-ROBBERS! WE'LL GO AFTER THE COUNTERFEITERS!

WALT DISNEY

70

IT LOOKS MORE LIKE MICKEY AND THE HAIR-ROBBERS HAVE EACH OTHER!

WELL, NOW WHAT'RE YA GONNA DO, KID?

THIS, FOR ONE THING!

AN' THEN THIS!

OKAY, DIPPY! YOU SLIP OUT WHILE I GOT 'EM COVERED!

GUARD THEM, DIPPY! I'M GONNA GET MORE WEAPONS! THEN WE'LL HEAD HOME!

HMMMMMM! WHICH ONES? WOW! I'VE GOT A GREAT IDEA!

NOW MARCH! AN' IF YA STOP, YOU'LL RUN THIS TORCH RIGHT AGAINST THE FUSE!

AND DIPPY STAYS TO GUARD THE EVIDENCE.

MEANWHILE, IN THE MAYOR'S OFFICE...

WHADDAYA MEAN WE AIN'T DONE NOTHIN'! WE'RE GETTIN' REAL CLOSE TO THOSE COUNTERFEITERS!

THAT'S NOT WHAT I HIRED YOU FOR!

YEAH! WE'RE LEAVIN' THE PUNKS TO DUMB-BELLS LIKE MICKEY MOUSE!

DUMB-BELL, HUH? JUST LOOK OUT THE WINDOW!

RAY! HURRAH!

WELL, MAYOR, THE HAIR-ROBBERS ARE SAFE IN JAIL AT LAST!

GREAT WORK, MICKEY!

YEAH! BUT WE'LL STILL GET THE COUNTERFEITERS!

LISTEN! IF YA DO TH' LITTLE THINGS, TH' BIG ONES SORTA TAKE CARE OF THEMSELVES!

IF YA PUT PENNIES IN THE BANK, YA WAKE UP WITH DOLLARS!

WHAT ARE YOU TALKIN' ABOUT?

PLENTY! YA SEE TH' HAIR-ROBBERS AN' TH' COUNTERFEITERS ARE TH' SAME GUYS! AN' WE CAPTURED THEM ALL!

DIPPY! YOU'RE SUPPOSED TO BE GUARDIN' THE EVIDENCE!

I DONE IT! ME AN' THE POLICE ROUNDED UP THE REST OF TH' GANG WHEN THEY CAME FOR THEIR STUFF!

THEY'RE WAITIN' T' TELL 'EM HOW LONG THEY GOTTA STAY HERE!

JAIL

DID YA PUT THE COUNTERFEIT MONEY IN A SAFE PLACE?

BOY, DID I?

SOLITARY CONFINEMENT

SEE, COULDN'T BE SAFER!

WELL, MICKEY, THE WHOLE TOWN IS PROUD OF YOU FOR SOLVING THE MYSTERY!

THANKS, MAYOR SCOTT!

HOW ARE YOUR TWO DETECTIVES?

THEY WERE PRETTY SORE WHEN I PUT THEM ON THE TRAIN!

YOU SEE, I PAID THEM OFF! BUT SINCE THEY WERE PHONY DETECTIVES,...

WHAT ABOUT?

I PAID THEM IN COUNTERFEIT MONEY!!

THE END

76

MICKEY MOUSE AND THE SACRED JEWEL

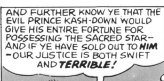

AND A LOT OF ANGRY MEN WITH KNIVES AND SPEARS ARE WAITING FOR MICKEY BELOW!

GEE! I'M SUNK!

AHUHAAA!!

CRRASH!

WELL, I'LL BE--I KNOCKED OUT THE WHOLE CREW!

BY GUM, MICKEY!

YEP! THEM GUYS ARE SURE OUT!

YEAH! BUT WE'RE STILL IN--AN' WE GOTTA SAVE MINNIE!

MAYBE THE QUICKEST WAY'D BE TO BUST THAT LOCK!

GOSH, DIPPY! GET BACK! SOMEBODY'S COMING!

CLICK! CLICK!

S-SHHH! BE SILENT AND FOLLOW ME!

GOSH! WHUR'S HE TAKIN' US?

SHH!

I DUNNO!

PSSST! THEES WAY!

IF WE ART DISCOVERED EET EES DEATH FOR ALL!

NOW LOOK!!

GOLLY!

THE SACRED STAR OF ZWOOSH!!

IF THOU WANTEST, I SELL EET TO YOU!

HOW COME YOU GOT THE SACRED STAR?

IT EES NO MATTER. KNOWEST I COULD SELL TO UNSCRUPULOUS PEOPLES BUT I RATHER HELP THOU!

HOW MUCH DO YOU WANT?

JUST FIVE HUNDRED SUMOLAHS!

HOW MUCH?

WE ONLY HAVE AMERICAN MONEY!

OH, IN AMERICAN MONEY, THAT EES EXACTLY FIFTEEN CENTS!

CAN IT BE THAT EASY TO GET BACK THE SACRED STAR?

IT IS WELL, OH SIR! THOU HAST ACTED WITH MANY WISDOM!

I AM HONORED! HERE IS YOUR MONEY, OH FRIEND!

GEE--WHAT A BREAK! WE GOT THE STAR!

THE HECK WE DID! Y' DON'T SUPPOSE I FELL FOR THAT GAG!

THEN THIS AIN'T...?

'COURSE NOT. LET'S FOLLOW THAT PHONY BIRD AND FIND OUT WHERE THE OTHER TWO HAVE MINNIE!

GOSH! WE'RE LOCKED IN AGAIN!

THIS IS ORFUL, MICKEY!

I BET THEY LOCKED US IN HERE T' STARVE!

HMMM! I WONDER ABOUT THAT PHONY BOX!

HEY! WHATCHA DOIN'?

GETTIN' US OUTTA HERE, I THINK! GET BACK, DIPPY!

BOOM!!!

JUST WHAT I THOUGHT--TH' RATS!

OHH-H! WHAT'S THAT?

THAT WAS THE FINISH OF THY PESKY FRIEND! NOW YOU'RE GOING ON A NICE LONG CAMEL RIDE!

WALT DISNEY

I ASK THEE - IS THAT AGED OR ISS IT AGED!

IT'S SWELL! I'LL TAKE THREE BARRELS!

BOY, I HOPE THIS WORKS, DIPPY!

SMELLS PRETTY DARN POTENT, B' GOSH!

IT'S NO GOOD, MICKEY. SHE'S NOT TAKIN'.

I WONDER WHAT ELSE I COULD PUT IN THERE!

AND SUDDENLY MICKEY GETS A GREAT IDEA!

A TRACTOR OUGHTA BE ABLE TO FLY ON THIS MIXTURE!

GARLIC SOUP

BLOOP

HOORAY, MICKEY! IT WORKED!

BLOOP

GET IN QUICK, MICKEY! SHE'S RUNNIN' WILD!

HOLD ON, DIPPY!

IT LOOKS MORE LIKE MICKEY IS THE ONE WHO NEEDS TO HOLD ON!

THET GAS HAS GOT TH' SHIP BUCKIN' LIKE A BRONCO!

PHEW-W! I PRETTY NEAR DIDN'T MAKE IT!

SHE'S FLYIN' FINE NOW, B' GOSH!

YEAH! WE GOTTA CATCH UP TO THOSE BIRDS IN A HURRY!!

AND WHAT OF THOSE TWO BIRDS? AND WHAT OF POOR MINNIE?

THOU ART LUCKY NOT TO HAVE BEEN BLOWN TO BITS WITH THY FRIEND!

I DON'T BELIEVE MICKEY WAS KILLED!

CANST BELIEVE THY EARS, BROTHER? CAN IT BE..?

DRAT IT! HE COULDN'T HAVE ESCAPED!

IT'S MICKEY! I KNOW IT!

IT IS, INDEED, MICKEY COMING TO THE RESCUE!

I SEE 'EM STRAIGHT AHEAD MICKEY!

DON'T SHOOT, DIPPY! YA MIGHT HIT MINNIE!

QUICK! WE DURST NOT LET THEM PASS!

THE STUPID RAT WON'T STAY DEAD!

BANG! BANG!

THEY GOT US, MICKEY! WE'RE DROPPIN'!

WE'RE NOT LICKED YET!

THEY MAY NOT BE LICKED, BUT IT SURE LOOKS BAD FOR MICKEY AND DIPPY!

HYAR! HYAR! THERE GOEST THY RESCUER LEETLE BLOSSOM!

YOU FIENDS!

THOU SAIDST IT! HEH! HEH! HEH!

AND MICKEY HAS LOST CONTROL OF THE DAMAGED PLANE, AND IS HEADING FOR A CRASH!

OH GOSH! WE'RE DONE FOR!

HANG ON, DIPPY! WE'RE GONNA HIT!

WHAT CAN SAVE OUR TWO FRIENDS?

WAIT! IN CASE THEY DOST STILL LIVE, WHAT AN ACT OF KINDNESS TO LEAVE "OLD SOAKH" HERE FOR 'EM!

MOST EXCELLENT IDEA, BROTHER!

GOOD-BYE, FOOLS!

GOSH, IT'S RIDIN' THE SAND LIKE A SLED!

WOTTA LANDING, MICKEY!

HOORAY, WE'RE SAVED!

SAVED, THE HECK! HOLD ON TO SOMETHIN'!

86

WHAM!

GOOD GOSH! WHAT A CRASH!

ARE YA DEAD, DIPPY?

I DUNNO YET, MICKEY!

WELL I GUESS WE'RE OKAY, BUT THAT SURE FINISHES OUR BLIMP!

HEY, LOOKIT, MICKEY! A CAMEL!

WITH THE CAMEL, MICKEY AND DIPPY STILL HAVE A CHANCE TO CATCH THE ROBBERS! AND TO SAVE POOR MINNIE!

SEEMETH TO ME THAT LAST CRASH DIDDEST OUR FRIEND!

IF IT DIDN'T HE GETTETH NOT FAR ON THE DOPEY CAMEL WE LEFTETH BEHIND!

C'MON, CAMEL! WE'LL GET 'EM YET!

HEY, WHAT'S WRONG WITH YOU? WHY DON'T YOU MOVE?

MEBBE HE DON'T TALK OUR LANGUAGE!

GOSH DANG! HE'S A REGLAR MULE, HE IS!

KEEP PUSHIN'! HE'S OUR ONLY CHANCE TO RESCUE MINNIE!

GOSH! LOOKIT HIS TONGUE HANGIN' OUT! SEE IF YA CAN GET SOME WATER OFFA THE BLIMP, DIPPY!

CAREFUL WITH THAT WATER, BOYS! THIS IS ONE STRANGE CAMEL YOU'RE DEALING WITH!

HERE Y' GO! DRINK IT ALL UP NOW!

I BET IT'S JUST WHAT HE NEEDED.

HE'S WALKIN' LIKE A DRUNKEN SAILOR, B'GOSH!

I NEVER HEARD O' GETTIN' DRUNK ON WATER!

WHAT'S THET, MICKEY?

GOSH! IT LOOKS LIKE A FILLIN' STATION!

HOW MANY, OH MASTER?

FILL HIM UP! HE'S CROCKED OR SOMETHIN'.

LAST CHANCE CAMEL FILLING STATION

A RARE SIGHT! NEVER DIDST I SEE AN INEBRIATED CAMEL BEFORELY!

YEAH! WELL HE BETTER SNAP OUT OF IT PRETTY QUICK!

WATER

HE'S DRUNKER'N EVER, MICKEY!

C'MON, LET'S GO NOW!

HIC!

HOW WILL OUR TWO FRIENDS EVER CATCH UP TO THE ROBBERS AT THIS RATE?

OH, NO! HE'S GOIN' IN CIRCLES!

WHAT AN ANIMAL!

HIC!

SINCE THEY HAVE NO CHOICE, MICKEY AND DIPPY CONTINUE TO WALK AROUND IN CIRCLES WITH THE DRUNKEN CAMEL!

WHILE MILES AND MILES AHEAD, THE ROBBERS SET UP CAMP!

NAUGHT TO DO NOW, BUT AWAIT THE COMING OF KASHDOWN AN' COLLECT!

RIGHT THOU ART!

SINCE THE GAME IS UP, OUR LEETLE FLOWER SHOULD KNOW WHO WE ART!

VERILY THOU HAST SAID IT!

WHO CARES, YOU BEAST!

PEGLEG PETE! AND SHYSTER! YOU VILLAINS!

POOR MINNIE! WHAT A SHOCK!!

HAW! HAW! HAW! I'M QUITE AN ACTOR, AIN'T I? I GOT TALENT AS WELL AS BEIN' HANDSOME!

NOT A SIGN OF KASH-DOWN YET! I WISH HE'D COME AN' TAKE THAT PESKY JEWEL OFF OUR HANDS!

HE PROMISED TO BE HERE TONIGHT!

I HOPE HE DON'T COME *TOO SOON*—I GOT SOME IDEES OF ME OWN!

OH, MICKEY WHERE ARE YOU?

THAT'S A VERY GOOD QUESTION, MINNIE!

PSSST! THUR'S FOLKS AHEAD!

IT'S A CARAVAN! MAYBE WE CAN MAKE A DEAL FOR A NEW CAMEL!

AND SO MICKEY AND DIPPY APPROACH THE STRANGERS...

I BRING YOU GREET-INGS, OH TRAVELER!

GREETINGS! WE'RE IN A HURRY AND WE NEED A NEW CAMEL!

BUT THE BEER MERCHANT KNOWS THEIR CAMEL WELL AND HE TELLS THEM THIS STORY!

IF THOU'RT IN HASTE, THOU NOW SITTETH ON *THE FASTEST CAMEL* IN THE DESERT! HIS NAME IS "OLD SOAKH"! HE LIVED ON BEER WHEN A KITTEN AND...

STILL FLOURISHETH ON THE SAME! BUT WATER MAKETH HIM COMPLETELY DRUNKEN!

WHADDYA KNOW ABOUT THAT!

FER GOSH SAKES!

BOY! WHAT A *DIFFERENCE*!

I'LL SAY! I BET WE CATCH THOSE ROBBERS *NOW*!

RACING THROUGH THE NIGHT, MICKEY AND DIPPY SOON COME UPON AN ISOLATED TENT IN THE DESERT!

WHUT DO WE DO NOW?

YOU WAIT HERE! I'M GOIN' TO DO A LITTLE SNOOPIN'!

WHAT A SURPRISE IS IN STORE FOR MICKEY WHEN HE PEEKS IN THE TENT!

AMAZED AT WHAT HE SEES, MICKEY LISTENS TO THE TWO CROOKS TO HEAR THEIR PLAN.

YUH BETTER GIT USED T'ME BEBBY! IF MICKEY AIN'T KILT HE A LONG WAYS FROM HERE!

THE BLAZES WITH MICKEY! WHERE THE DICKENS IS *KASH-DOWN* WITH OUR DOUGH!

F'GOSH SAKES! PETE AND SHYSTER! AND THEY GOT A DATE WITH PRINCE KASHDOWN! DOGGONE IT!

WOTCHA WORRIED ABOUT, SHYSTER? KASHDOWN'LL BE ALONG—AN' *NUTHIN'* KIN HAPPEN TO US *HERE*!

OH NO? MICKEY SURE LOOKS LIKE HE HAS SOME-THING UP HIS SLEEVE!

HEY, DIPPY! THOSE TWO NATIVES WE'VE BEEN CHASIN' ARE PETE AND SHYSTER IN DISGUISE!

YUH MEAN WE BEEN CHASIN' THE WRONG GUYS?

WHUT'S THIS DISGUISE FOR, MICKEY?

YOU'RE PRINCE KASH-DOWN AND I'M YOUR GRAND VIZIER! HERE'S WHAT WE'RE GONNA DO!

MICKEY EXPLAINS THE PLAN TO DIPPY, AND A SHORT TIME LATER...

I ART THE GRAND VIZIER IN THE SERVICE OF HIS MAGNILOQUENT ROYALNESS, PRINCE KASHDOWN!

THY MOST GRANDIFEROUS HIGH-NESS, THESE BE THE GAZABOS WHO STOLETH THE SACRED STAR FOR THEE.

VARLETS! PIGS! HOW DAREST THEE APPEAR-EST BAREHEADED BEFORE ME? 'TIS AN INSULT! 'TIS B'GOSH!

HONEST, PRINCE, WE DIDN'T MEAN NUTHIN' UNGENTEEL!

CERTAINLY *NOT!* WE 'ER MUST HAVE MISLAID OUR TURBANS AND WE HAVE NOTHING TO COVER OUR HEADS!

BUT MICKEY AND DIPPEY DIDN'T COME ONLY TO TALK ABOUT ETIQUETTE!

TRY THESE FOR SIZE!

1935

MICKEY'S PLAN HAS WORKED!!

HAW! HAW! BOY, DID I MAKE A SWELL PRINCE!

YEAH, DIPPY! THEY SURE FELL FOR IT!

AND WITH PETE AND SHYSTER OUT OF THE WAY...

OH, I'M SO HAPPY I COULD CRY! THEY TOLD ME YOU WERE DEAD!

YEAH? WELL, IT WAS A BAD GUESS!

MINNIE IS SAVED!!

AND NOW FOR THE STAR OF ZWOOSH!

HERE'S THE STAR! LET'S GET OUTTA HERE QUICK! KASHDOWN'LL BE HERE ANY MINUTE!

MICKEY IS SO RIGHT!

NAME OF THE DEVIL! HOW MUCH FARTHER DO WE HAVE TO GO?

BUT A FEW HUNDRED CAMEL STRIDES, THY NOBLE HIGHNESS!

MICKEY AND HIS FRIENDS BETTER HURRY!!

C'MON! LET'S GET GOIN'!

SHOULDN'T WE ORTER TAKE "OLD SOAKH" ALONG?

NO, WE DON'T NEED HIM! AND HE'LL BE TOO DRUNK FOR ANYBODY TO CHASE US WITH!!

HE'S SOBER ENUFF NOW!

YEAH! BUT AS SOON AS HIS BEER WEARS OFF HE'LL BE DRUNK AS A LOON!

THEY'RE OFF! AND JUST IN THE NICK OF TIME, TOO!

CURSES! METHINKS THERE HAST BEEN FOUL PLAY!

YOU BETTER BELIEVE IT, PRINCE KASHDOWN! AND MICKEY'S GETTING FURTHER AWAY BY THE MINUTE!

IT AIN'T FAIR! HE HIT ME WHEN I WASN'T LOOKIN'!

WE WERE TRICKED! WE THOUGHT IT WAS YOU!

GET UP QUICKLY, YOU BUNGLING DOGS!

AFTER THEM! THEY MUST BE CAUGHT ERE THEY REACHETH RAGHBAGH!

I'M GONNA WRING THUH LITTLE RAT'S NECK!

HOLD THY TONGUE! CATCH FIRST A BIRD, ERE THOU COOK IT!

MICKEY, MINNIE, AND DIPPY HAD BETTER RIDE LIKE THE WIND NOW THAT PRINCE KASHDOWN IS IN PURSUIT!!

I HOPE WE CAN GET TO RAGHBAGH AND GET THE SACRED STAR TO THE CALIPH OF UMBRELLASTAN BEFORE KASHDOWN CAN STOP US!

THINK THEY'RE GONNA FOLLER US, MICKEY?

DARN RIGHT! WISH THESE CAMELS HAD A HIGH GEAR OR SOMEP'N!

MEANWHILE, WHAT OF POOR CAPTAIN CHURCHMOUSE?

THE TWO MOONS OF GRACE ARE SOONLY EXPIRED, NOBLE CAPTAIN!

TH' TIME AIN'T UP YET, YE BLASTED SCUM!

WE BEG YOU TO COMETH WITH US NOW!

OH GOSH! HERE THEY COME! AND THEY'RE GAININ' ON US WITH EVERY STRIDE!

HOW FER IS RAGHBAGH?

I DUNNO! BUT THEIR CAMELS ARE MUCH FASTER THAN OURS!

RAGHBAGH
STUMBOOL

HA! THEIR CAMELS WEAKEN! WE SHALT TAKE THEM ERE THEY REACH THE GATES!

BUT THE CITY COMES INTO SIGHT JUST THEN!!

YIPPEE! WE'RE SAFE!

WE'RE NOT IN THERE YET, DIPPY!

MICKEY HAD BETTER DO SOME FAST TALKING!!

MICKEY, MINNIE, AND DIPPY MAKE IT SAFELY THROUGH THE GATES OF RAGHBAGH AND ONCE AGAIN PETE AND SHYSTER ARE FOILED!

THE TELEGRAM IS SPEEDING TO AMERICA BUT THE MINUTES ARE TICKING BY ALL TOO QUICKLY!

AND THE TWO EMISSARIES ARE WAITING WITH GREAT ANTICIPATION TO EXECUTE POOR CAPTAIN CHURCHMOUSE!

WORLD-WIDE CABLEGRAM

SACRED STAR DELIVERED BY MICKEY MOUSE. NOT NECESSARY FOR KILL CAPTAIN NOW. RETURN UMBRELLASTAN TO ONCELY. HOUV-YA-BEN

P.S. PLEASE PAY DOBERMAN FOR AIRSHIP. I WRECKED IT. MICKEY

CONCLUSION

MICKEY AND MINNIE ARE AS UNSELFISH AS EVER WITH THEIR FRIENDS!

EVIDENTLY, ACCORDING TO THE CALIPH, THERE WAS A GRAIN OF RADIUM INSIDE THE STONE BUT HE DOESN'T LET HIS PEOPLE KNOW! THEY THINK IT'S A LUCKY STAR. AND, MICKEY CONCLUDES...

THE END

MICKEY MOUSE AND PLUTO THE RACER

MICKEY MOUSE AND PLUTO THE RACER

SATURDAY DAWNS AT LAST—THE DAY OF PLUTO'S DEBUT AS A RACER! AND HE'S RARIN' TO GO!

GOIN' TO THE RACE, HORACE?

YOU BET! I'M JUST SPOILIN' FOR A GOOD LAUGH!

YOU MEAN THIS—THIS—IS GOING TO RACE?

IMPOSSIBLE! WE WON'T HAVE IT!

HERE'S HIS ENTRY COUPON!

HIS PAPERS ARE O.K.— WE'VE GOT TO LET HIM IN!

IT'S A DISGRACE! AND ON OUR OPENING DAY, TOO!

YOU WAIT! PLUTO'S GOIN' TO BE THE SENSATION OF THIS RACE!

THAT'S WHAT I'M AFRAID OF!

WALT DISNEY

NO	DOG	ODDS
1	FLEA CIRCUS	4 to 1
2	LADY O'GRADY	3 to 5
3	BEEF STEW	3 to 2
4	HOT FOOT	6 to 5
5	PEDICULOUS	8 to 3
6	RUFF ON KATZ	8 to 1
7	HAMBONE	10 to 1
8	PLUTO	286 to 1

286 TO 1! AND THEY SAY THEY KNOW DOGS. PHOOEY!

SOME ODDS!

HAW! HAW!

FIRST TIME YOU RACED, HUH SON?

UH, YES, IT IS!

WE'D LIKE TO WISE YUH UP TO SOMETHIN'!

YUH SEE—YUH DIDN'T PUT LIGHTS ON THIS PUP'S HARNESS!

LIGHTS!? BUT IT'S DAYTIME!

YEAH! IT'S AWFUL IMPORTANT!

YEAH! BUT IT'LL BE PLENTY DARK WHEN HE GETS TO THE FINISH LINE!

HAW! HAW! HO! HO! THAT'S A GOOD ONE!

THE MAIN EVENT OF THE DAY IS ABOUT TO START! THE BAND STRIKES UP, AS THE PROUD OWNERS PARADE THEIR DOGS TO THE STARTING BOX!

TWEEDLEDY! BLAAAAA!! OOMPAH!

HOT DOG HOORAY!

'RAY!

C'MON, PLUTO! GET IN THAT PARADE AND LOOK DIGNIFIED!

HAW! HAW! HO HAW! HAW! HA! HA! HA! HA! HA!

WALT DISNEY

GET IN THERE, PLUTO! THE RACE STARTS FROM HERE!

I AIN'T HAD SO MUCH FUN SINCE UNCLE JOB SWALLERED HIS STORE TEETH!

BOY! THIS IS A RIOT, NOT A RACE!

LISTEN TO THE CROWD! THEY THINK IT'S A COMEDY!

IT'S ALL YOUR FAULT, SHOEBUCKLE! YOU SIGNED THE ENTRY BLANK!

JUDGES

I DIDN'T HAVE THE HEART TO REFUSE! THE KID WAS SO PROUD OF THAT MUTT!

WELL, IF THAT DOG MAKES ANY MORE TROUBLE, YOU'RE FIRED!

BACK TO THE RACE! THE DOGS ARE ALL SET, THE ELECTRIC RABBIT IS ON ITS WAY, AND WHEN THE STARTING DOOR SPRINGS UP, THE RACE WILL BE ON!

REMEMBER, PLUTO, WHEN YOU SEE THAT RABBIT— RUN!!

WOOF! WUF!

—MOST BRILLIANT FIELD OF CANINE RACERS THAT EVER TOED THE MARK! —THE RABBIT IS OUT! HE'S TEN YARDS AWAY! TWENTY! THIRTY! THERE GOES THE DOOR! THEY'RE OFF!

PLUTO! F'GOSH SAKES! GET GOIN'!

POOR MICKEY! PLUTO DOESN'T SEEM TO KNOW WHAT IT'S ALL ABOUT!

PLUTO! CHASE THAT RABBIT! SIC 'IM!

HA! HAW! HA! HA!

GOOD GRIEF! THE WHOLE CROWD'S LAUGHING AT THAT MUTT!

THEY'RE NOT EVEN WATCHING THE RACE!

NUMBER 8, OWNED BY MICKEY MOUSE, HAS HAD STARTER TROUBLE! HE'S JUST NOW UNDER WAY—HALF A LAP LATE IN A TWO-LAP RACE! WHAT A PUP!

"WHAT'S EVERYBODY SO DARNED EXCITED FOR? THERE'S NO SENSE IN RUNNIN' WITH-OUT A REASON!"

95

It looks like Zowie has just **GOT** to win that race! He's a pretty important dog right now!

GEE, YOU'RE IN A SPOT, MR. SHOE-BUCKLE! WHAT IF ZOWIE DOESN'T WIN?

He **SHOULD** WIN! I'VE CLOCKED HIS TRIALS AND THERE ISN'T A **DOG** AT THE TRACK THAT CAN BEAT HIM!

Y'KNOW, MR. SHOE-BUCKLE, EVER SINCE PLUTO MESSED UP THAT RACE, WE GET THE HORSE LAUGH FROM EV'RYBODY— AND— I WAS WONDERIN'—!

YES?

WELL, MAYBE YOU COULD TRAIN HIM WITH ZOWIE —JUST ENOUGH SO'S PEOPLE WOULDN'T LAUGH!

SURE, MICKEY! I DOUBT HE'LL EVER WIN A RACE, BUT HE'LL LEARN TRACK MANNERS AND REDEEM HIMSELF!

SHAKE, PARTNER! WE'LL SHOW 'EM!

Pluto's **FIRST** DAY OF TRAINING HAS ARRIVED!

READY, MICK-EY! LET'S GO DOWN TO THE TRACK FOR A WORK-OUT!

GEE, I FORGOT! THE COMMITTEE WON'T LET PLUTO AND ME ON THE TRACK!

THAT'S RIGHT! YOU WERE BARRED!

YEAH! AND YOU LOST YOUR JOB ON THE COMMITTEE!

BUT I'M STILL A MEMBER, AND THEY CAN'T STOP ME FROM RACING!

I GOT IT! PLUTO AND ME WILL BE WORKIN' FOR YOU AS TRAINER AND HANDLER!

WHAT **NERVE**! THEY TOLD ME YOU WERE HERE! LEAVE THESE GROUNDS INSTANTLY!

JUST A MINUTE! I'VE GOT A RIGHT TO BE HERE WITH MY DOG!

YES! **YOU** HAVE! BUT NOT **THIS** HALF-WITTED KANGAROO!

YOU BE CAREFUL WHAT YOU CALL MY DOG!!

ANYHOW HE'S NOT COMPETING! HE'S A RUNNING MATE FOR ZOWIE!

H-MMPH! IT'S ALL **VERY** IRREGULAR!

WELL, WE GOT AWAY WITH THAT! NOW LET'S HAVE A GOOD TRAINING SESSION!

KANGAROO! HALF-WITTED! WHO IS HE TO CALL PLUTO NAMES!?

GEE! ZOWIE SURE IS **FAST**!

I JUST HOPE HE'S FAST ENOUGH TO WIN THE RACE!

GOSH, MR. SHOEBUCKLE! HE'S JUST GOT TO WIN THE SWEEP-STAKES!

YES, MICKEY! IT'S THE ONLY WAY I CAN SAVE MY HOME!

HMMM! PRETTY GOOD TIME! AND HE'LL BE FASTER AGAINST COMPETITION!

LOOK! PLUTO CROSSED THE LINE, TOO! HE WENT ALL THE WAY 'ROUND! YIPPEE!

SAY, WHYN'T YUH GIT A GOAT FER A RUNNIN' MATE —HE'D BE MORE COMPETITION!

IF I **HAD** A GOAT, YOU'D GET IT!

JUST 'CAUSE ZOWIE'S FAST— DON'T MEAN THAT PLUTO'S NOT FAST, TOO!

HAR! HAR! YUH MEAN FAST TO TH' GROUND!

PLUTO **IS** A FAST DOG!

I'LL BET HE AIN'T EVEN FAST COLOR!

THAT'S WHY HE CAN'T **RUN**!

AW! WHY AM I WASTIN' TIME ON YOU BIRDS?

HAW! HAW! HAW!

And, in fact, from daily practice with Zowie, Pluto **IS** GETTING BETTER. BUT HE STILL CAN'T CATCH THE RABBIT!

"I'M GETTIN' SICK OF HAVIN' THAT THING GET AWAY EV'RY TIME!"

"THERE MUST BE SOME WAY TO CATCH IT!'"

"I GOT IT! I'LL HEAD IT OFF!

BONG!!

OH, PLUTO! AN' YOU WERE GETTIN' SO GOOD!

WELL, HE WON'T DO IT AGAIN!

96

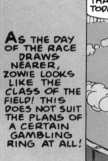

97

98

100

101

MICKEY MOUSE RUNS HIS OWN NEWSPAPER

MICKEY MOUSE RUNS HIS OWN NEWSPAPER

ⓞNE DAY MICKEY WAS WALKING DOWN THE STREET, WHEN SOMETHING MADE HIM STOP IN HIS TRACKS!

THE DAILY **WAR DRUM** FOR SALE VERY CHEAP INCLUDING GOOD WILL AND FIXTURES

HMMM! MINNIE'S ALWAYS PESTERIN' ME TO SETTLE DOWN IN A QUIET BUSINESS! I WONDER!

WELL, IT WON'T DO ANY HARM TO GO IN!

WHAT CAN I DO FOR YOU?

I WAS WONDERIN' ABOUT BUYIN' YOUR PAPER! IT'D HAFTA BE **REAL** CHEAP!

MY FRIEND! IT'S SO CHEAP YOU CAN NAME YOUR OWN PRICE!

GOSH! WHY IS IT SO CHEAP?

I'VE BEEN SLAMMING AT THE GANGSTERS AND POLITICIANS WHO HAVE BEEN GETTING INTO THIS TOWN!

YOU MEAN, THE RACKETEERS ARE AFTER YOU?

THAT'S THE TRUTH, YOUNG MAN! THEY SURE ARE!

MAKE OUT THE BILL! HERE'S THE FIRST PAYMENT!

THANKS! THE PAPER IS YOURS! TAKE MY ADVICE, DON'T TRY ANY CRUSADING!

SO MICKEY HAS BOUGHT THE "**DAILY WAR DRUM**"! AND AFTER A FEW DAYS INSTRUCTIONS FROM THE FORMER OWNER, HE IS READY TO TAKE OVER!

I HOPE I DO O.K.!

YOU WON'T HAVE TROUBLE UNLESS YOU TRY EXPOSING GRAFT LIKE I DID!

HELLO, MINNIE! LOOK AROUND!

MICKEY! OH, ISN'T IT SCRUMPTIOUS! JUST THINK! YOU'RE THE OWNER AND **EVERYTHING** OF A REAL NEWSPAPER!

EV'RYTHING IS RIGHT! LOOK! THE **PORTER** CLEANS OFF A CHAIR SO THE **PRESIDENT'S** GIRL FRIEND CAN SIT DOWN!

I'M SO PLEASED! I THINK IT'S THE **GRANDEST** THING!

NOW I NEED TO GET SOME HELP!

RIGHT HERE, M'BOY! Y' SEE TWO OL' NEWSPAPER MEN RARIN' TO GO TO WORK!

THE LAST SHOP I WORKED IN THREW THEIR LINOTYPES AWAY, 'CAUSE I COULD SET A STICK O' TYPE FASTER'N THEY COULD!

O.K., FELLERS! YOU'RE ON!

AN' WHAT CAN YOU DO, DIPPY?

WELL, I GOT A CAMERA AN' A NOSEY DISPOSITION— AN' I C'N **CUSS** LIKE THE DICKENS!

WITH HORACE AS PRESSMAN AND DIPPY AS REPORTER AND CAMERAMAN, THE WHEELS OF MICKEY'S VENTURE BEGIN TO TURN!

McSNOOP, FROM FROM THE "MORNING PRESS"! I HEARD THE "WAR DRUM" CHANGED HANDS SO I DROPPED IN!

WHADDYA WANT TO KNOW?

THE USUAL! WELCOME TO THE FOLD STUFF! NAMES OF OWNERS, PUBLISHERS, EDITORS! FUTURE POLICY OF THE RAG!

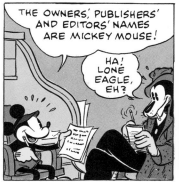

THE OWNERS', PUBLISHERS' AND EDITORS' NAMES ARE MICKEY MOUSE!

HA! LONE EAGLE, EH?

AND OUR POLICY IS TO PRINT THE **TRUTH!** NO CORRUPT POWER CAN DICTATE—!

YEH! I KNOW! BUT BETWEEN OURSELVES WHAT GROUP ARE YOU STRINGIN' WITH?

106

MICKEY, SOMETHING OUGHT TO BE DONE ABOUT THE ERRORS IN THE PAPER! MRS. VAN BUZEM JUST CANCELED HER SUBSCRIPTION!

DIDN'T WE GIVE HER BRIDGE PARTY A BIG SPREAD— PHOTOGRAPH AND ALL?

THE ARTICLE AND PHOTOGRAPH WERE GREAT—

!

BUT THE HEADLINE BELONGED ON THE **SPORTS PAGE**!

HEAVYWEIGHTS WILL BATTLE TONIGHT

I CAME TO SEE IF YOU HAD THE ACCOUNT OF MY DAUGHTER'S WEDDING CORRECT! I AM **VERY** PARTICULAR!

I HOPE YOU MENTIONED THAT HER TRAIN WAS HELD UP BY FOUR FLOWER GIRLS!

HERE'S THE EARLY EDITION, MRS. UPPAKRUST! WE PUT IT ALL IN!

THE HAPPY COUPLE

BRIDE'S COSTUME

YOU MAY CANCEL MY SUBSCRIPTION **IMMEDIATELY**!

WALT DISNEY

WHERE YA GOIN', MICKEY?

I'M GOING TO INTERVIEW JUDGE BULL! HE'S GOT A NEW CAMPAIGN ON AUTO DRIVERS, AN' I WANTA GET THE DOPE ON IT!

PRESS CAR

HEY, PULL OVER! WHERE D'YUH THINK YUH'RE GOIN' IN SUCH A HURRY!

I'M ON MY WAY TO COURT TO INTERVIEW JUDGE BULL!

YOU **SURE** ARE! I'M GONNA ESCORT YUH—**PERSONAL**!

EXTRA! DAILY WAR-DRUM! SPECIAL EXTRY!

THE WAR-DRUM?!!

MUCH OBLIGED, KIDDO!

HEY! THAT'S FIVE CENTS!

YEAH? WELL SUE ME FOR IT!

BET THE "BOSS" DON'T KNOW THIS SHEET'S RUNNIN' AGAIN!

COME BACK HERE AN' **FIGHT**!

JUS' DROPPED IN TO OFFER YUH SOME HELP!

YESSIR?

SORRY, BUT WE DON'T NEED ANY HELP!

YES YUH DO! THERE'S MOBS THAT WRECK JOINTS LIKE THIS HERE!

BUT FOR, SAY—TWENTY BUCKS A WEEK YUH C'D HAVE PERFECTION!

GET OUT OF HERE **FAST**, OR I'LL BEND A CHAIR OVER YOU!

BETTER THINK IT OVER, SPORT! SOME OF THEM MOBS IS PERTY **TOUGH**!

MICKEY IS BEGINNING TO SEE WHAT HE'S UP AGAINST!

QUICK, DIPPY! I WANT Y' TO TRAIL SOME-ONE!

HUH, MICKEY! WHO?

HE'S WEARIN' A PLAID OVER-COAT AN' A DERBY— HE WON'T KNOW **YOU**—PHONE IN WHERE HE GOES!

PLAID DERBY!—TELEPHONE ME!— **I GOT IT**!

I DON'T GIT WHY I'M DOIN' THIS, BUT I HOPE IT'S FRONT PAGE!

Y'SEE, WE GOTTA FIND WHO'S **BE-HIND** THIS BIRD—THEN WE'LL EXPOSE THE WHOLE DARN RACKET!

YEAH! WE'LL LEARN 'EM THE POWER OF THE PRESS!

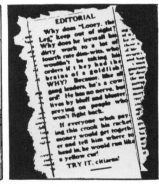

111

MICKEY MOUSE AND THE PIRATE SUBMARINE

MICKEY MOUSE AND THE PIRATE SUBMARINE

120

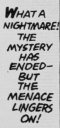

I'LL HAVE TO DO IT THIS WAY! I SURE HOPE TH' SUBMARPLANE WORKS!

HERE GOES A *TRY* AT IT!

BANG!

MICKEY IS OFF! THE SUBMARPLANE IS *IN THE AIR*— ON ITS MAIDEN VOYAGE!

GOOD GOSH! THE WINGS ARE FOLDIN' UP FROM THE PRESSURE! WHAT DO I DO *NOW?*

MICKEY HAD BETTER FIGURE OUT HOW TO OPERATE THE SUBMARPLANE *QUICKLY!!*

G-GOSH!

WHAT LEVER DO I PULL *NOW?*

NOPE! WRONG AGAIN!

WHOOPEE! *THAT'S* THE ONE! AN' SHE *WORKS!*

NOW I GOTTA HURRY UP AN' FIND DOCTOR VULTER'S SUBMARINE!

LEMME SEE—HE HEADED OUT SORTA WESTERLY— WITH AN HOUR'S HEAD-START! I OUGHTA PICK HIM UP IN ABOUT—

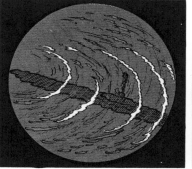

HOT DIGGETY! IT'S THE SUBMARINE ALL RIGHT!

BUT— NOW THAT I'VE *FOUND* IT—WHAT AM I GONNA DO?

DOGGONE! I CAN'T RADIO FOR HELP 'CAUSE VULTER WOULD SURE PICK UP THE MESSAGE!

I CAN'T *ATTACK* IT ON ACCOUNT OF GLOOMY AN' THE CREW ABOARD! I JUST GOTTA FOLLOW 'EM *!!*

THEY'RE HEADED FOR THAT ISLAND! BUT THERE'S *NO PLACE* T' LAND! LOOKIT THOSE CLIFFS! THEY'LL BE *WRECKED!*

WELL, I'LL BE— IT RAN RIGHT INTO THE CLIFFS—AN' DIS-APPEARED!

DOCTOR VULTER'S SUBMARINE BECOMES MORE MYS-TERIOUS ALL THE TIME!

I *KNOW* IT HIT THAT CLIFF AN' YET THERE'S NO SIGN OF A WRECK!

MAYBE IT'S CAUGHT ON A LEDGE AN' NOT BADLY DAMAGED! I'LL HAVE TO—

— GO DOWN AN' *LOOK* FOR IT!

BOY! THIS 'UD BE *FUN,* IF IT WASN'T FOR GLOOMY AN' THE CREW BEIN' IN *DANGER!*

HMMM—IT'S FUNNY! DOCTOR VULTER SEEMED TO KNOW *EXACTLY* WHERE HE WAS GOIN'!

WHOOPEE! I THINK I SEE IT AHEAD!

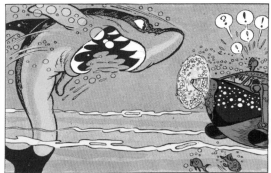

NOPE! WRONG AGAIN!

FINDING NO TRACE OF THE PIRATE SUBMARINE, MICKEY DECIDES TO EXPLORE THE UNCHARTED ISLAND !!

GOSH! THOSE CLIFFS MUST BE A THOUSAND FEET HIGH! AN' THEY RUN CLEAR AROUND THE ISLAND!

THAT'S FUNNY! IT'S NOT SOLID AT ALL! IT'S HOLLOW—LIKE A CRATER!

F' GOSH SAKES! AN' I THOUGHT IT WAS UN-INHABITED!

THIS BEATS ME! I FIND A WHOLE MODERN CITY ON AN UNCHARTED ISLAND!

GOSH! I NEED GAS! I HOPE THEY HAVE A "WELCOME" SIGN OUT AN' MAYBE SOMEONE CAN TELL ME MORE ABOUT DOCTOR VULTER!

THERE'S ONLY ONE WAY TO FIND OUT!

HEY! *SWELL!* THEY'RE COMIN' OUT T' *MEET* ME!

LET'S HOPE THEY'RE REALLY HERE TO **WELCOME** *YOU, MICKEY !!*

IF I ONLY KNEW WHAT HAPPENED TO DOCTOR VULTER'S PIRATE SUBMARINE, I'D BE SITTIN' ON TOP OF—

HEY! WHAT TH' HECK!

WELL! F' GOSH SAKES!

MICKEY IS SURE ON TOP OF **SOMETHING!** *UNFORTUNATELY, IT'S DR. VULTER'S SUBMARINE, WHICH CAME UP RIGHT UNDER HIM !!*

WELL, MY FOOLISH FRIEND, AND WHERE DID YOU COME FROM?

AND HOW'D *YOU* GET HERE?

YOUR PLANE! I SAW IT ON THAT SHIP! YOU WERE HIDING! YOU SAW ME CAPTURE IT!

SURE I DID! AN WHAT'S MORE, I—

CAPTAIN, ARREST THIS SPY *IMMEDIATELY!*

YES, YOUR MAJESTY!

BOY! *WHAT A SPOT TO BE IN!*

THERE ARE A FEW QUESTIONS I WOULD LIKE TO ASK YOU!

YEAH? AN' I'VE GOT A COUPLE FOR YOU, TOO!

WHY WERE YOU ON THAT SHIP—SPYING ON ME?

SPYING? HONEST, DR. VULTER I TRIED T' LET YA KNOW I WAS THERE—BUT YA GOT AWAY BEFORE I HAD A CHANCE!

HOW MUCH DO YOU KNOW OF MY PLANS FOR *CONQUERING THE WORLD!?*

SO *THAT'S* WHAT—I MEAN-G-GOSH! I DIDN'T EVEN *KNOW* YOU WERE GOIN' T' CONQUER IT!

WELL, *I AM!* AND WHAT IS MORE—*YOU* ARE GOING TO HELP ME!

WHAT CAN DOCTOR VULTER POSSIBLY MEAN BY THAT ?

HEY, WHERE ARE YA TAKIN' ME?

YOU HAVE BEEN ASSIGNED TO WORK IN DR. VULTER'S FARM LANDS!

BUT— BUT— I'M NO FARMER!

THAT'S WHAT YOU THINK! PICK UP THAT HOE— AND GET TO WORK!

THE GUARD GOES AWAY, LEAVING MICKEY CHAINED TO ANOTHER "FARMER"!!

I WONDER WHAT'S HAPPENED TO GLOOMY AND THE REST OF TH' CREW!

YUH NEEDN'T WONDER! I KNOW'D YOU'D SHOW UP—SOONER OR LATER!

WELL, FER—IT'S GLOOMY!

MICKEY AND GLOOMY START COMPARING NOTES—TRYING TO FIND OUT WHAT HAPPENED—AND WHY—AND HOW!

WE'RE IN TROUBLE UP TO OUR NECKS, MICKEY! VULTER'S MECHANICAL WIZARD!

YUH OUGHTA SEE THAT SUBMARINE O' HIS! AN' TH' ELECTRO-MAGNET HE STOPPED THE SHIP WITH!

AN' THAT'S HOW HE CAN CAPTURE 'EM WITHOUT HURTIN' 'EM!

EASY! TH' LAKE EXTENDS BELOW SEA LEVEL! HE RUNS THROUGH A TUNNEL WHICH STARTS IN THAT CLIFF— AN' ENDS IN TH' LAKE!

BUT HOW'D HE GET HIS SUBMARINE ONTO THIS ISLAND?

WHY SURE! I MUST BE DUMB NOT THINKIN' OF THAT!

WELL, VULTER AIN'T! AN' DON'T YOU FORGET IT!

BUT GLOOMY—WHAT'S DR. VULTER PLANNIN' TO DO?

HE'S GONNA CONQUER TH' WORLD—AN' B'GOSH, I B'LEEVE HE CAN DO IT!

THIS ISLAND'S A SWELL HIDEOUT! A SHIP'D NEVER GUESS WHAT WAS HERE! AN' IF THEY GOT TOO NOSEY—HE'D SINK 'EM!

BUT WHY IS HE CAPTURIN' ALL THESE PRISONERS?

PRISONERS NUTHIN'! WANTA KNOW WHAT THAT GUY IS DOIN'?

HE'S SHANGHAI-ING HIS WHOLE ARMY!!

GLOOMY, NO MATTER HOW IMPOSSIBLE IT SEEMS, WE GOTTA ESCAPE FROM THIS PLACE!

SHHH! HERE COMES A GUARD!

BASED ON YOUR EXPERIENCE, YOUR ABILITY, AND YOUR MENTAL RATING, DR. VULTER HAS GIVEN YOU PERMANENT JOBS!

GLOOMY GOES TO THE AIRPLANE FACTORY! AND YOU—COME WITH ME—TO THE PALACE!

THE PALACE! SWELL! S'LONG, GLOOMY!

MENTAL RATING! ABILITY! EXPERIENCE! FOOEY!

OF ALL THE CHEESY, DEGRADIN' JOBS! GLOOMY AN' I JUST GOTTA FIND A WAY OUTA HERE!

BRRRT—3-RRRT— BRT— BRRRRRT— BRRT

HEY! THAT SOUNDS LIKE CODE! I WONDER...

MICKEY LEAVES HIS CHORES AND GOES TO THE WALL TO LISTEN!

IT IS CODE! A COUPLE OF SHIPS AT SEA—TALKIN' TO EACH OTHER! TH' RADIO ROOM MUST BE RIGHT NEXT DOOR TO TH' KITCHEN!

BRT— BRT·BRT· BRRRRRT— BRT— BRT!!

MICKEY IS HAPPILY LISTENING TO THE RADIO, WHEN THE SOUND OF A NOISY WASHING MACHINE DROWNS IT OUT!

HEY! WHY DON'T YA OIL THAT?

WHY? I LIKE TH' NOISE!

WHIR-R-R-R! GRONK! GRRR-ANK!

WELL, IT'S GOTTA BE OILED! OR I'LL GO—

NOW YOU'VE DONE IT! THAT'S DR. VULTER'S PERSONAL LAUNDRY!

TH' MOTOR'S COLD, BUT THERE'S NO TIME T' WARM IT UP!

I'LL SAY THERE'S NOT! THEM SOJERS IS GETTIN' CLOSE!

RIGHT, MICKEY! THE GUARDS ARE RIGHT ON YOUR TAIL!!

O.K.— WE'RE OFF!

BANG! BANG! BANG!

BANG!

CLIMB 'ER FAST, KID! REMEMBER THAT RIM IS LINED WITH GUNS

ENEMY PLANE RISIN'!

MAN TH' GUNS!

LET 'EM HAVE IT!

THERE'S 100 MANY OF 'EM! THEY COULDN'T MISS! WE'RE AS GOOD AS DEAD!

SO LONG, PAL! IT'S BEEN SWELL DYIN' WITH YUH THIS WAY! I KNOW YUH DONE YER BEST!

AW, SHUT UP AN' SIT DOWN!

THERE'S STILL A CHANCE, GLOOMY!

WELL, THERE GOES TWO MORE WHO TRIED TO OPPOSE DR. VULTER--TH' NITWITS!

LITTLE DO THEY KNOW THAT THE LITTLE PLANE TURNS INTO A SUBMARINE UNDER THE WATER!

BUT NOW MICKEY AND GLOOMY MUST SEARCH FOR DR. VULTER'S SUBMARINE TUNNEL TO ESCAPE FROM THE ISLAND!

YUH DON'T EVEN KNOW WHERE IT IS! YER CRAZY! WE'LL BE KILLED!

WE'D HAVE BEEN KILLED IF WE DIDN'T TRY IT! THAT'S FOR SURE!

I THINK IT'S SOMEWHERES OVER AT THIS END O' TH' LAKE!

TURN ON TH' SEARCHLIGHT! WE GOTTA TAKE A CHANCE!

I THINK THEY'VE SEEN US, MICKEY! YUH BETTER FIND THAT TUNNEL QUICK!

THERE IT IS, GLOOMY!

HOT DIGGETY! WE MADE IT!

SEE, GLOOMY! IT'S GETTIN' LIGHTER UP AHEAD!

HOORAY! IT'S TH' OCEAN!

MICKEY AND GLOOMY HAVE DONE THE IMPOSSIBLE — THEY'VE ESCAPED FROM DR. VULTER'S ISLAND! THERE'S CAUSE TO CELEBRATE!!

WHOOPEE! WE'RE SAFE!!

WELL, IF WE'RE SAFE, WHY TH' BLAZES DON'T YUH ACT LIKE IT!

DO YUH THINK WE'LL CATCH UP WITH 'EM?

YEAH, GLOOMY! THEY DON'T HAVE THAT MUCH OF A HEAD START ON US!

MICKEY! LOOK! DOWN BELOW— A PERISCOPE!

HOW DO YUH KNOW IF IT'S DR. VULTER'S SUBMARINE?

I DON'T KNOW!

BUT I BETCHA A HUNDRED BUCKS I FIND OUT!

RATA TAT TATA TAT TAT TA TAT—

SWOOPING DOWN ON THE SUBMARINE, MICKEY SHOOTS OFF ITS PERISCOPE WITH HIS MACHINE GUN

NICE SHOOTIN', KID!. A BULLS-EYE!

THAT TRICK SHOULD BRING THE SUBMARINE TO THE SURFACE— NO MATTER WHOSE IT IS !!

NOW WE'LL SEE IF WE GOT TH' RIGHT SUBMARINE! LOOK, GLOOMY! IT'S COMIN' UP NOW!!

EVERY MAN TO HIS POST! ANTI-AIRCRAFT GUN CREWS ON DECK! IF IT'S FIGHT THEY WANT, WE'LL GIVE IT TO THEM!

V-1

OUR MACHINE GUN'S ABOUT AS USEFUL AS A PEA-SHOOTER AGAINST THEM WEAPONS! BUT WE GOT A TORPEDO!

TH' MECHANISM'S ALL SET! IT CAN'T MISS! YOU RAM IT INTO THE TUBE AN' I'LL RELEASE IT!

TELL ME WHEN GLOOMY! SHE'S ALL READY! LET HER GO AS SOON AS I—

—TELL YUH !!

AIMING THE TORPEDO TO SCORE A DIRECT HIT ON DR. VULTER'S SUBMARINE, MICKEY RELEASES THE MECHANISM TOO SOON!

HOW CAN GLOOMY GET OUT OF THIS ONE !?

HELP! HELP! GOOD GOSH! WHAT HAVE I DONE?

GLOOMY! LET GO! YOU'LL BE KILLED !!

I CAN'T! I'M SURROUNDED!!

POOR GLOOMY! WHAT-EVER HE DOES, HE'S LOST!

I KNOWED SUMP'N' LIKE THIS 'UD HAPPEN! SOMEBODY DO SUMP'N'! QUICK!

HE CAN'T LET HER GO OR TH' SHARKS'LL GET 'IM! AN' IF HE HANGS ON— OMIGOSH!

TORPEDO! JUMP FOR YOUR LIVES!

POOR GLOOMY! HE'S DONE FOR! I CAN'T LOOK!

WHOOPEE! I'M SAVED!

IT'S A MIRACLE! GLOOMY MANAGED TO DROP THE TORPEDO WHEN A HUGE WAVE SHOT IT OVER THE SUBMARINE!

BOY! AM I HAPPY !! YOU, SIR, ARE MY PRISONER!

PRISONER NUTHIN'! I'M YOUR SLAVE !!

WHOOPEE! WHAT A LUCKY BREAK! WITH GLOOMY SAFE, ALL I HAFTA DO IS—

GOSH SAKES! HOW AM I GONNA SINK TH' SUBMA-RINE WITHOUT SINKIN' GLOOMY, TOO?

MICKEY HAD BETTER THINK OF ANOTHER PLAN PRETTY QUICKLY !!

DR. VULTER DOESN'T KNOW TH' SUBMARPLANE CAN DIVE AS WELL AS FLY! AN' THAT GIVES ME MY ONE CHANCE!

THEY'RE SHOOTIN' NOW! IF HE THINKS HE HIT ME, MAYBE I CAN SNEAK UP ON HIM FROM BELOW!

WE GOT HIM! NICE SHOOTIN'! THERE HE GOES!

CHART ROOM! PROCEED AT HALF SPEED TO THE "S.S. BORZOW"! WE SHALL CAP-TURE IT TONIGHT!

130

THAT HOLE IS JUST ABOUT GOING TO FINISH DR. VULTER AND HIS CREW!

NOW, T' GET UP ON THE SURFACE AN' SEE WHAT HAPPENS!

WHOOPEE! IT WORKED! I'VE GOT 'EM! I'VE WON!

EVERYBODY THROW YER GUNS OVERBOARD! YOU FRISK 'EM, GLOOMY!

NOW GET OUT TH' LIFEBOATS QUICK! TH' SUBMARINE IS SINKIN' FAST!

BUT WE HAVE NO LIFE-BOATS!

GOOD GOSH! WHAT'RE WE GONNA DO? YA CAN'T ALL DROWN!

BUT MICKEY CAN ALWAYS BE DEPENDED ON TO COME UP WITH A PLAN!

QUICK! RIP UP THE DECKS! WE'VE GOTTA BUILD A RAFT!

GRAB THIS LINE AN' HAUL THESE TOOLS ABOARD! GLOOMY, YOU TAKE CHARGE!

GOOD WORK, GLOOMY! HOP ABOARD! TH' REST OF YA PILE ON TH' RAFT!

THERE SHE GOES!

RIDE 'EM COWBOYS! WE'RE HEADED FOR YOUR LA-AA-AST ROUNDUP!

WITH THEIR PRIZE IN TOW, MICKEY AND GLOOMY HEAD TOWARD THE STEAMER BORZOW!!

SMOKE AHEAD, MICKEY! AN' IF THAT AIN'T TH' BORZOW, I'LL EAT IT— SMOKESTACK AN' ALL!

GOSH, MINNIE! IT LOOKS LIKE— IT IS! IT'S THE SUB-MARPLANE!

WHAT IS IT, CAPTAIN DOBERMAN?

MICKEY!

HI, FOLKS! GOIN' OUR WAY!

BOY, O' BOY! I'M SURE GLAD T' SEE YA!!

CAPTAIN DOBERMAN, SIR! THE MYSTERIOUS 'S' WAS A PIRATE SUBMARINE! WE SANK IT—AND CAPTURED THE CREW!

STEP ABOARD, MICKEY! LET ME BE THE FIRST TO CON-GRATULATE YOU!

OH, NO, CAPTAIN!!

YOU CAN BE SECOND!

THE END

MICKEY MOUSE AND THE FOREIGN LEGION

MICKEY MOUSE AND THE FOREIGN LEGION

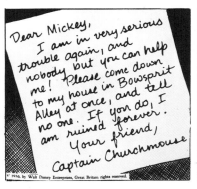

YEAH, MICKEY MOUSE! KIDNAPED! RIGHT OFF TH' STREET! TH' ONLY CLEW IS A JOCKEY CAP HE WORE! YEAH! O.K., I'LL WAIT!

THERE'LL BE A HUNDRED MEN ON TH' TRAIL IN AN HOUR! THEY'RE SENDIN' OUT A COUPLE O' BLOODHOUNDS! DON'T WORRY— WE'LL FIND 'IM!

IN WITH 'IM, JOE! WE'VE GOT NO TIME T' LOSE!

AN' IF YUH MOVE A MUSCLE, I'LL PLUG YUH— UNNERSTAND?

THIS IS WHERE MICKEY WAS KIDNAPED! HERE'S HIS CAP!

O.K.— WHIFF IT GOOD, SNOOP-NOSE! LEAD US TO HIM!

CAN A BLOODHOUND REALLY FIND SOMEBODY JUST BY SMELLING HIS CAP?

SNOOPNOSE CAN!

HOGAN'S LIVERY STABLE

ROWRF! OURF! OURF!

I'LL TAKE HIM INSIDE! YOU GET RID O' THAT CAR— QUICK!

HERE HE IS, CHIEF!

HMMM! SORT OF A RUNT, ISN'T HE? I THOUGHT HE'D BE BIGGER! TAKE OFF HIS GAG, JOE!

SEEMS T' ME YOU GUYS ARE GOIN' TO A LOT OF TROUBLE T' STEAL 25 BUCKS!

THAT'S NOT WHY YOU WERE BROUGHT HERE!

I SIMPLY WANT YOU TO ANSWER ONE EASY QUESTION! IF YOU DO, YOUR LIFE WILL BE SPARED!

GEE IT'S BIG-HEARTED OF YA! WHAT'S TH' QUESTION?

WHERE DOES CAPTAIN DOBERMAN KEEP THE PLANS FOR HIS NEW AIRPLANE?

YOU HEARD ME! NOW ANSWER THE QUESTION!

WHY DO YA WANTA KNOW? WHO ARE YOU? WHAT'S TH' IDEA?

I'LL ASK THE QUESTIONS HERE! AND IF YOU DON'T ANSWER— YOU'LL NEVER LEAVE THIS HOUSE ALIVE!

NOW I KNOW I'LL NEVER TELL YA!

IF TH' SECRET'S THAT IMPORTANT— YER WASTIN' TIME ASKIN' ME FOR IT!

O.K., MEN! PREPARE THE "PERSUADER"!

NOW, MY FRIEND! YOU HAVE JUST ONE MINUTE TO TALK—OR ELSE!

WHAT ARE YA REALLY TRYIN' T' DO— SCARE ME OR KID ME?

YOU'RE NOT AFRAID, EH?

WHY SHOULD I BE? YOU'RE NOT GONNA SHOOT! IF ALL YA WANT FROM ME IS INFORMA-TION, YOU'RE NOT GONNA GET IT THAT WAY!

PERHAPS NOT, MY FRIEND! BUT THERE ARE OTHER WAYS! LET ME SHOW YOU!

NOW, WE'LL JUST STRETCH YOU OUT—UNTIL YOU DECIDE TO TALK! IT SHOULDN'T TAKE LONG!

I DON'T CARE WHAT YA DO—I'LL NEVER TELL YA ABOUT CAPTAIN DOBERMAN'S PLANE!

DON'T BE TOO SURE ABOUT IT, MY FRIEND!

HEY! OWOOOOOO! THAT TICKLES! CUT IT OUT! CUT IT—CUT —CUT IT OUT!

HE SOUNDS MORE LIKE A CHICK-EN THAN THE HEN DOES!

GOLLY! THAT'S MORE'N TWO QUARTS OF GRAIN ALREADY! THAT'S ENOUGH— YOU CAN STOP NOW!

SO! YOU'VE GIVEN UP NOW, EH?

NO! TH' CHICKEN HAS!

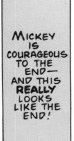

144

AND SO MICKEY GETS READY TO LEAVE ON HIS **MISSION**, THOUGH HE IS SOMEWHAT RELUCTANT TO GO!

BUT IT'S 200 MILES! WHY CAN'T I EVEN TAKE A CAMEL?

YUH CAN'T SNEAK UP ON ANYBODY RIDIN' A CAMEL! **YUH GOTTA WALK!**

BUT, PETE! I CAN'T CARRY ENOUGH FOOD! OR WATER! OR **ANYTHING!**

THAT'S YOUR PROBLEM! YUH VOLUNTEERED, DIDN'T YUH? NOW GIT GOIN'!

NICE WORK, PETE! **THAT'S** SURELY THE END OF MICKEY!

YEP! FER GOOD! C'MON, LET'S CELEBRATE!

ASHES TO ASHES. DUST TO DUST. IF THE NATIVES DON'T GET HIM, THEN THE DESERT MUST!

AFTER TWO DAYS, WITH 170 MILES TO GO, MICKEY IS EXHAUSTED, HIS FOOD IS NEARLY GONE, AND—

WELL—THAT'S THAT! NO MORE WATER! AN' I COULD DRINK A **BARREL** OF IT—IN ONE GULP!

WHAT A **SWELL** OUTLOOK! IF I GO BACK, I'LL GET SHOT FOR DISOBEYIN' ORDERS! AN' IF I GO ON, I'LL STARVE T' DEATH!

PETE **REALLY** WANTED T' GET RID OF ME—AN' I GUESS HE FIGGERED THAT THIS 'UD BE TH' SUREST WAY T' DO IT!

WELL—ALL I CAN SAY IS— **HE WAS RIGHT!**

MEANWHILE, BACK AT THE FORT, PETE IS SUMMONED BEFORE THE COLONEL!

I'VE HEARD THAT YOU SENT PRIVATE MICKEY MOUSE OUT ON A 200 MILE WALK IN THE DESERT! IS THAT RIGHT?

YES, SIR! THAT'S RIGHT, SIR!

THEN YOU'RE GUILTY OF EXCEEDING YOUR AUTHORITY, OF MALICIOUS PERSECUTION AND OF GROSS NEGLIGENCE!

OH, YES, SIR! THANK YUH, SIR! THAT'S JUST WHAT I THOUGHT TOO!

AND WHAT'S MORE—YOU GO AFTER HIM AND YOU BETTER BRING HIM BACK ALIVE, OR I'LL HAVE YOU COURT-MARTIALED AND SHOT FOR **MURDER!** UNDERSTAND?

WHY TH' BLASTED, SLAB-SIDED, TWO-HUMPED SWAB! WHAT DOES HE THINK I AM—A **PRIVATE!?**

TH' TROUBLE IS I'M TOO SOFT-HEARTED FER MUH OWN GOOD!

INSTEAD O' SHOOTIN' 'IM LIKE I SHOULD O' DONE, I GAVE 'IM A CHANCE TUH DIE OUT ON TH' DESERT ALL BY HIMSELF, SLOW AN' PEACEFUL-LIKE!

GOOD GOSH! **THERE HE IS!** PASSED OUT! I HOPE I'M NOT TOO LATE!

HEY, YUH BLASTED LITTLE SWAB! **WAKE UP!** DON'T DIE ON ME—OR I'LL GIT IN TROUBLE!

AW, MICKEY, YUH LITTLE RAT—PLEASE DON'T DIE NOW! CAN'T YUH HEAR ME? IT'S YER OLD FRIEND, PEGLEG PETE!

I'VE COME TUH TAKE YUH BACK NOW, SEE? AN' I FORGIVE YUH FER EVERYTHING YUH EVER DONE TUH ME BEFORE!

YUH **CAN'T** DIE, KID! YUH GOTTA COME TUH LIFE! I JUST COULDN'T STAND TUH GO BACK THERE **WITHOUT** YUH!

CAUSE IF I **DID**—TH' COLONEL SAID HE'D HAVE ME **SHOT!**

SO YUH AIN'T GONNA GO AN' DIE NOW, ARE YUH?

GIMME ANOTHER DRINK OF WATER—AN' HELP ME ONTO YOUR HORSE—THEN MAYBE I'LL BE OKAY!

THERE! NOW I'LL GIT YER PACK AN' CLIMB ON BEHIND YUH!

THAT'S A GOOD IDEA!

BUT I'VE GOT AN EVEN BETTER ONE! SINCE YOU'RE TH' GUY WHO MADE ME WALK OUT HERE—

LET'S SEE HOW **YOU LIKE WALKIN' BACK!** SO LONG, PETE!

WE'LL SEE HOW PETE LIKES HIS HIKE BACK! IT SERVES HIM RIGHT AFTER SENDIN' ME OUT T' STARVE T' DEATH! ONLY—

DOGGONE IT! HE'D NEVER MAKE IT! AN' I COULDN'T LET ANYBODY GO THROUGH WHAT I DID!

WELL, YUH CAME BACK FER ME! I'M A COCK-EYED CAMEL!

YOU'RE WORSE THAN THAT! BUT GET ON ANYWAY!

I'M SURE GLAD I HATE YUH! 'CAUSE IF I DIDN'T I'D LIKE YUH! AN' I DON'T WANNA LIKE YUH 'CAUSE I HATE YUH TOO MUCH!

© 1936, by Walt Disney Enterprises, World rights reserved.   6-13

IT'S A GOOD THING YUH CAME BACK FER ME—OR YOU'D BE PUSHIN' UP DAISIES REAL SOON!

WELL— ANYWAY —ONE OF US WOULD BE!

HOW FAR IS IT TO TH' FORT NOW?

I DUNNO! I S'POSE NINE OR TEN MILES!

GOOD! THAT'S RIGHT WHERE I HOPED WE WERE!

IT'S JUST FAR ENOUGH T' GIVE YOU AN IDEA OF WHAT IT WAS LIKE FER ME!

© 1936, by Walt Disney Enterprises, World rights reserved.   6-15

WHEN PETE FINALLY REACHES THE FORT, HE AND MICKEY ARE SUMMONED TO APPEAR TOGETHER BEFORE THE COLONEL!

THANK YOU, SERGEANT! I'VE HEARD YOUR STORY, AND I'LL HANDLE THIS CASE MYSELF! DISMISSED!

PRIVATE MOUSE: YOU DELIBERATELY MADE THE SERGEANT WALK TEN MILES ACROSS THE DESERT! DO YOU THINK THAT IS THE WAY TO SHOW PROPER RESPECT FOR A SUPERIOR OFFICER?

N-N-NO, SIR!

FOR YOUR ACTION, YOU SHOULD BE PUNISHED—AND PUNISHED SEVERELY! THIS IS OFFICIAL! DO I MAKE MYSELF CLEAR?

Y-Y-YES, SIR!

GOOD! THEN, UNOFFICIALLY— JUST BETWEEN OURSELVES — I THINK THE BIG DOPE GOT JUST WHAT HE DESERVED!

© 1936, by Walt Disney Enterprises, World rights reserved.

TH' COLONEL'S TAKIN' MY SIDE AGAINST PETE WAS SURE A SWELL BREAK— 'CAUSE NOW PETE'LL BE SCARED TO PICK ON ME SO MUCH!

WHAT'S MORE, I FINALLY HAVE TIME T' DO SOME DETECTIVE WORK!

FIRST—I'VE GOTTA LOCATE THOSE STOLEN GUN PLANS! AN' I'VE GOT A HUNCH THEY'RE HIDDEN IN PETE'S QUARTERS!

WELL—IT'S TAKIN' A BIG CHANCE—BUT THERE'S ONLY ONE WAY T' FIND OUT!

© 1936, by Walt Disney Enterprises, World rights reserved.   6-18

IF MY HUNCH IS RIGHT I JUST GOTTA FIND PETE'S HIDIN' PLACE—

NOW WHERE WOULD THEY BE? AN' I HAVEN'T GOT ANY TIME T' WASTE!

LEMME SEE! IF I WERE HIDIN' 'EM, WHERE'D I PUT 'EM? I KNOW! I BETCHA THEY'RE UNDER THE MATTRESS!

© 1936, by Walt Disney Enterprises, World rights reserved.

HOT DIGGETTY! NOW I'VE GOT PETE AN' TRIGGER RIGHT WHERE I WANT 'EM! I'VE GOT PROOF!

CLUMP! CLOP! CLUMP! CLOP!

GOOD GOSH! SOMEBODY'S COMIN'!

C'MON IN, TRIGGER! SET DOWN!

© 1936, by Walt Disney Enterprises, World rights reserved.

I'VE GOT A SCHEME TUH GIT US OUT O' HERE WITH THESE PLANS—AN' GIT RID O' MICKEY MOUSE IN TH' BARGAIN!

147

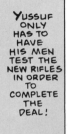    

I AM VERY HAPPY! FOR YEARS, THEY HAVE BEEN CALLING ME THE "SCOURGE OF THE DESERT"—NOW I CAN BECOME ITS KING!

I WILL LOOT, AND MASSACRE, AND PLUNDER AND PILLAGE UNTIL THE DESERT FLOWS RED, AND PEOPLE TREMBLE WHEN THEY HEAR MY NAME!

AND ALL BECAUSE YOU SOLD ME THESE RIFLES! IT WAS A GREAT FAVOR! I WILL NEVER FORGET IT! AND NOW, MY FRIEND— BEFORE IT IS TIME FOR US TO PART—

I'LL TAKE BACK THE THREE THOUSAND DOLLARS I PAID YOU!

WHY-WHY- YOU BIG!

LET US NOT AR- GUE—OR I MAY CHANGE MY MIND AND KILL YOU AFTER ALL!

I AM GLAD TO FIND THAT YOU ARE WISE AS WELL AS SHREWD! FAREWELL, MY FRIEND! MAY GOOD FORTUNE ATTEND YOU!

THE DOUBLE- CROSSING, CROOKED, MURDERING CHISELER!!

YEAH! YOU SAID IT!

AN' HE DOESN'T KNOW IT—BUT HE'S ALSO AN AWFUL SUCKER!

YOU MUST HURRY! IT WILL BE DARK BEFORE YOU REACH THE SERGEANT'S CAMP!

YEAH! AN' I'M COUNTIN' ON IT BEIN' DARK BEFORE YUSSUF AIPER GETS BACK TO HIS CAMP, TOO!

NOW, TAKE TH' CARAVAN AN' WAIT TILL YA HEAR FROM ME! AN' THEN— YOU COME A-HUSTLIN'!

SO LONG, PIEKH ABOU! AN' THANKS!

FAREWELL! MAY GOOD LUCK AND PEACE BE WITH YOU!

WELL—THAT'S A NICE WISH— BUT IF GOOD LUCK FOLLOWS ME, I WON'T HAVE ANY PEACE! NOT WHERE I'M GOIN'!

WALT DISNEY

AND SHORTLY AFTER NIGHTFALL, MICKEY APPROACHES THE OASIS WHERE PEGLEG PETE IS CAMPED WITH THREE SQUADS OF LEGION- NAIRES!

I SURE HOPE I MADE IT BACK IN TIME! 'CAUSE IF THERE'S A SLIP—MY LIFE'S NOT WORTH A PLUGGED PENNY!

HALT! WHO GOES THERE?

PRIVATE MOUSE REPORT- ING FOR DUTY, SIR!

TRIGGER, IT'S HIM!

LET'S GO! TUHNIGHT'S TH' NIGHT! AT LAST WE'VE GOT THAT RAT WHERE WE WANT 'IM!

PRIVATE MICKEY MOUSE REPORTING FOR DUTY, SIR!

WELL, IT'S ABOUT TIME! GO GIT CORPORAL HANK! I WANTA SEE 'IM!

CORPORAL! ME AN' PRIVATE HAWKES IS GOIN' OUT ON A SCOUTIN' TRIP! YOU'RE IN COMMAND WHILE I'M GONE!

YES, SIR!

AN' DON'T WORRY ABOUT NUTHIN'! WE'LL BE BACK TOMORROW!

I'LL SAY WE'LL BE BACK TOMORROW!

AN' WE'LL BRING 'EM A FEW VISITORS, IN CASE THEY GIT LONESOME! HAW! HAW!

CORPORAL! DOUBLE TH' SENTRY! WAKE TH' MEN AT MID- NIGHT TO REPORT FOR BATTLE! THEN I'LL LAY OUT TH' PLANS!

PLANS? BATTLE? WHO DO YOU THINK YOU ARE?

LISTEN YOU BLASTED, DUMB- WITTED PRIVATE, DIDN'T YOU HEAR THE SERGEANT SAY I WAS IN CHARGE WHILE HE'S GONE!?

OH! RIGHT! I FORGOT!

FROM TH' COLONEL!

YES, LIEUTENANT MOUSE!

151

152

HE WAS RIGHT BESIDE ME WHEN WE REACHED THE CAMP!

WHERE COULD HE HAVE GONE? WHO SAW HIM LAST?

I DID! WHILE THE TRIBE WAS WRECKING THE CAMP, HE SLIPPED AWAY AND RODE ACROSS THE DESERT! HE PASSED BY NOT TWENTY FEET FROM ME!

WELL, FER GOSH SAKES— WHY DIDN'T YA SHOOT 'IM?

I COULDN'T, LIEUTENANT!

YOU SAID—NO MATTER WHAT HAPPENED— NOBODY WAS TO FIRE UNTIL YOU GAVE THE COMMAND!

DOGGONE TH' COCKEYED LUCK! ALL MY HARD WORK WAS FOR NUTHIN'! HE GOT AWAY AS CLEAN AS A WHISTLE!

THE DOUBLE-CROSSING APE!

BUT I'D FEEL A LOT WORSE IF HE'D HAD THOSE BLUEPRINTS WITH HIM!

WHAT?!

YA MEAN— HE HASN'T GOT 'EM?

YOU THINK I'D LET THAT DOUBLE-CROSSER CARRY 'EM? NOT A CHANCE! I STOLE 'EM FROM HIM IN THE SHEIK'S CAMP!

HERE! I HOPE THEY'LL DO YOU MORE GOOD THAN THEY DID ME!

LIEUTENANT MOUSE, SIR! THE COLONEL HAS JUST ARRIVED— WITH A DETACHMENT OF SOLDIERS!

HOT DIGGETTY! THAT IS — I'LL REPORT AT ONCE!

YOU COME WITH ME, TRIGGER! I'M KEEPIN' MY EYES ON YA, FROM NOW ON!

WHAT'S THE LEGION GONNA DO WITH ME NOW, MICKEY? SHOOT ME?

NOT A CHANCE! I'M TAKIN' YA BACK HOME! AFTER THAT, IT'S UP TO TH' DEPARTMENT OF JUSTICE!

HMM — I GUESS THIS ADDS A CHAPTER TO THE OLD STORY! CRIME DOESN'T PAY!

WELL, MAYBE NOT A WHOLE CHAPTER! BUT IT'LL ADD AT LEAST A SENTENCE!

LIEUTENANT MOUSE, SIR! REPORTING THAT YOUR ASSIGNMENT HAS BEEN COMPLETED!

YUSSUF AIPER AN' HIS BAND ARE DISARMED! I WAS ABLE TO RECOVER TH' PAPERS I WAS AFTER—AN' I CAPTURED TH' THIEF WHO STOLE 'EM!

ALL THERE IS LEFT T' DO IS SEND A DETACHMENT OF TROOPS TO TH' SHEIK'S CAMP— AN' PICK UP TH' REST O' TH' RIFLES AN' AMMUNITION!

CONGRATULATIONS, MY LAD! AND TO THINK YOUR VICTORY WAS ACHIEVED WITHOUT ANYONE GETTING INJURED!

WELL, PRACTICALLY, SIR! I THINK A COUPLE OF GUYS HAD THEIR FEELINGS HURT PRETTY BAD!

THERE'S ONLY ONE PLACE WE SLIPPED UP, COLONEL! SOMEHOW, OR OTHER, PEGLEG PETE GOT AWAY FROM US!

I KNOW! DON'T WORRY ABOUT IT!

HE IS A DESERTER AND A CRIMINAL! WE WILL OFFER A BIG REWARD FOR HIS CAPTURE— DEAD OR ALIVE!

HE WILL NEVER BE RETURNED TO YOU! AND NO REWARD WILL EVER BE PAID!

WHADDAYA MEAN?

HE DOUBLE-CROSSED MY TRIBE! SOMEDAY THEY WILL FIND HIM! AND THAT IS ALL THE REWARD THEY WILL NEED!

I PROMISED THAT IF YOU DID THIS JOB, YOU COULD NAME YOUR OWN REWARD! SO—GO AHEAD! YOU'VE CERTAINLY EARNED IT!

WELL — AS YOU KNOW I'M REALLY A SECRET SERVICE AGENT! I ONLY JOINED TH' FOREIGN LEGION BECAUSE I WAS AFTER TRIGGER HAWKES!

SO — NOW THAT I'VE GOT 'IM— I'D LIKE T' GET OUT OF TH' LEGION— SO'S I CAN TAKE 'IM BACK HOME— T' JAIL!

I'M SORRY TO LOSE YOU, MICKEY! THE FOREIGN LEGION NEEDS MEN LIKE YOU! BUT A PROMISE IS A PROMISE! I'LL ARRANGE IT FOR YOU!

THE NEXT DAY, BACK IN DASSIS ALI- MICKEY HAS OBTAINED HIS DISCHARGE AND IS READY TO LEAVE FOR HOME!

GOOD-BYE, MY LAD! A GUARD OF HONOR WILL ACCOMPANY YOU AND YOUR PRISONER TO THE BOAT! ONCE ABOARD YOU WILL HAVE NO TROUBLE!

AND IF YOU EVER WANT TO COME BACK — I WILL BE PROUD TO HAVE YOU AS ONE OF MY OFFICERS!

THANK YA, SIR! AN' YA CAN'T TELL — MAYBE SOME DAY I WILL!

BUT BEFORE I GO — I WANT T' DO JUST ONE MORE THING!

WHAT?

I WANT T' SALUTE TH' SWELLEST OFFICER TH' FOREIGN LEGION EVER HAD!

SO MICKEY HAS FINISHED HIS STINT IN THE FOREIGN LEGION! HE SOON REACHES THE PORT OF AITA KLAH KURFU AND TAKES "TRIGGER" HAWKES ABOARD SHIP!

CAPTAIN! I WANT THIS PRISONER TO BE PUT INTO IRONS IMMEDIATELY— AN' KEPT THERE!

I'LL DO IT AT ONCE!

BO'S'N! I WANT YOU TO THROW THIS MAN IN THE BRIG! POST A SPECIAL GUARD OVER HIM— TWENTY-FOUR HOURS A DAY!

AYE, AYE, SIR!

THE SECRET SERVICE IS GOING TO HOLD YOU PERSONALLY RESPONSIBLE FOR HIM UNTIL WE REACH HOME!

YOU CAN PUT YOUR MIND AT REST!

THAT'S NOT ALL I'M GONNA REST FOR TH' NEXT WEEK!

FINALLY, AFTER A RESTFUL AND UNEVENTFUL VOYAGE, MICKEY'S SHIP DOCKS AT HOME! AND, AS HE WALKS DOWN THE GANGPLANK —

CAPTAIN DOBERMAN!

MICKEY, HOW ARE YOU, MY BOY?

GOLLY, BUT I'M GLAD T' SEE YA! IT WAS SWELL OF YA T' COME AN' MEET ME!

SWELL OF ME!? GREAT GRIEF! I'M PROUD TO MEET YOU! YOU'VE DONE A GRAND JOB, MY BOY!

YOU KNOW, MICKEY- WE DIDN'T HEAR FROM YOU IN SUCH A LONG TIME THAT WE'D JUST ABOUT GIVEN YOU UP!

I DON'T MUCH BLAME YA, CAPTAIN! FOR A WHILE THERE, I WAS ABOUT TO GIVE MYSELF UP!

HELLO, MAJOR!

MICKEY MOUSE! WELL, BLESS MY SOUL! COME IN! TELL ME HOW YOU DID IT!

IT WAS NUTHIN', SIR! I JUST OBEYED YOUR ORDERS! YA TOLD ME T' FIND TH' BLUEPRINTS AN' TH' GUY WHO STOLE 'EM — AN' BRING 'EM BOTH BACK, SO I DID!

THIS IS THE CASE CARD WHICH DESCRIBES THE ROBBERY! AND, EVEN THOUGH YOUR ADVENTURES WOULD PROBABLY FILL A BOOK, ALL I CAN WRITE HERE IS SIX WORDS—

BLUEPRINTS RECOVERED! PRISONER ARRESTED! CASE SOLVED!

WELL, SIR- AFTER ALL- WHAT MORE IS THERE TO SAY?

HERE ARE TWO CHECKS — ONE FOR THE MONTHS YOU'VE BEEN IN THE SECRET SERVICE, AND THE OTHER AS A REWARD FOR CAPTURING TRIGGER HAWKES!

GEE! THANKS, SIR!

GOOD-BYE, MY BOY! AND REMEMBER- THERE'S A JOB WAITING FOR YOU HERE- ANY TIME YOU WANT IT!

WHOOPEE! I'M RICH!

YESSIR! I WANT TH' BIGGEST BOX OF CANDY YOU'VE GOT!

GOODA DAY, MA'AM! I GOTTA SOME NICE-A THINGS, MEBBE YOU BUY, EH?

NO, THANK YOU! I WOULDN'T CARE FOR ANYTHING TODAY!

MEBBE SOME NICE-A FLOWERS?

THANKS— NO!

NO!

I SAID NO!

HE'SA VERY FRESH!

JOOSTA PICKED!

NOT EITHER SOME JEWELRY?

NO! CAN'T YOU HEAR?

NO! NO! NO!

HAH, I KNOW YOU WANNA BUY-A DA NICE FRESH CANDY, NO?

WELL— THEN HOW ABOUT A NICE FRESH YOUNG MAN?

MICKEY!

THE END

154

MICKEY MOUSE'S ADVENTURES WITH ROBIN HOOD

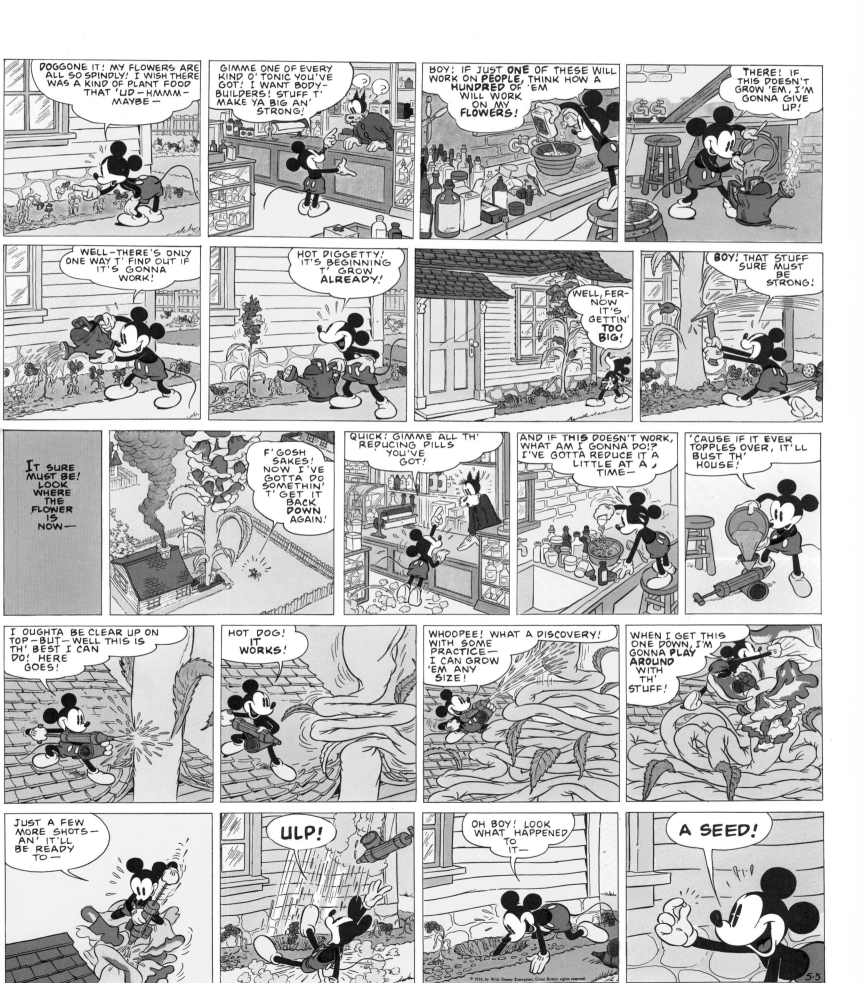

IT LOOKS LIKE MICKEY'S EXPERIMENT HAS BACKFIRED! WHAT WILL HE DO NOW?

HERE, PLUTO!

I KNOW I MUST LOOK SORT OF FUNNY!

BUT IF YOU JUST LET ME DOWN ON TH' FLOOR NEAR TH' TONIC, I'LL MAKE MYSELF BIG AGAIN!

FER GOSH SAKES! I FORGOT ALL ABOUT THAT FLY!

HUZZ! SOZZ YEZ ROZZ!

ZIZZIFIZIZ-ZZZ WOZZZ-Z-Z-Z-Z!

BRRRR

R-ROW-OOO!

LOOK! HE'S LAUGHIN'! WOZZ WOZZ WOZZ WOZZ WOZZ!

ATTA BOY, PLUTO! GO GET 'IM, BOY! AR-RRRR!

ZOZZ OWZZ! OZZ SOZZ YEZ WOZZ!

OWOOOOO!

PLUTO RUNS AWAY TERRIFIED, WITH THE HUGE FLY IN HOT PURSUIT!

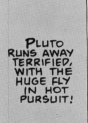

Robinson Crusoe

FLY PAPER

OF ALL TH' SILLY PICKLES T' BE IN! IF I WAS SOMEBODY ELSE I'D PROB'LY BE LAUGHIN' AT ME!

Robin Hood

BUT IT'S NO LAUGHIN' MATTER! I GOTTA GET TO TH' BASEMENT AN' GET BIG AGAIN!

GR-RRR-R-RRR!

WUZZ! WUZZ! WOZZ! WOZZ! WOZZ!

ZUZZ YEZ WUZZ, ZOZZ!

WOP!

F' GOSH SAKES! NOW I AM IN A JAM! WITH PLUTO GONE, HOW'LL I EVER GET OFF THIS TABLE?

Robin Hood

SOZZ! YUZZ ZOZZ HUZZ! WOZZ!

Robin Hood

AND SOON MICKEY IS TAKEN BEFORE THE SHERIFF OF NOTTINGHAM!

SIRE, WE HAVE TWO PRISONERS! THIS ONE WE CAUGHT POACHING ON HIS MAJESTY'S DEER

HANG THE SWINE AT ONCE!

THIS OTHER ONE IS A BALMY VARLET THE CHIEF FORESTER FOUND LURKING AROUND SHERWOOD FOREST JUST NOW!

SPEAK! WHO ART THOU? WHENCE CAMEST THOU?

I'M MICKEY MOUSE AN' I JUST POPPED IN FROM TH' TWENTIETH CENTURY!

I KNOW NOT THAT PLACE! WHERE IS IT?

WELL—IT'S REALLY EVERYWHERE—ONLY ABOUT A THOUSAND YEARS FROM NOW!

SO THOU KIDDEST ME, DOST THOU? TO THE DUNGEON WITH YOU!

YEAH!?

LISTEN, YOU OLD FOSSIL! I'LL TEAR YA RIGHT OUT OF TH' BOOK!

ENOUGH! HANG HIM WITH THE OTHER ONE!

GOSH! I DON'T REMEMBER THIS CHAPTER! I GOTTA THINK OF SOMETHIN'—QUICK!

LOOK! THAT PEDDLAR! IT'S ROBIN HOOD—IN DISGUISE!

AFTER HIM!

HOT DIGGETTY! IT WORKED! NOW'S OUR CHANCE!

CLIMB ABOARD!

THAT WAS NICE WORK, LAD! WHAT IS THY NAME?

MICKEY MOUSE!

I AM GLAD TO KNOW THEE! MINE IS ROBIN HOOD!

WALT DISNEY 6-21
© 1936, by Walt Disney Enterprises, World rights reserved.

WHAT A COINCIDENCE! MICKEY IS AMAZED AT HIS GOOD FORTUNE!

THY QUICK WIT SAVED MY LIFE, LAD! NOW I MUST REPAY THEE!

WILT THOU SERVE ME AND ENTER MY COMPANY OF MERRY MEN? WHAT SAYEST THOU?

OH BOY! OH BOY! I SAYEST IT'S SWELL!

HELLO, MY FRIENDS!

LOOK!

'TIS ROBIN HOOD!

HE'S TURNED BEGGAR!

A CLATTERING TINSMITH, ON MY HONOR!

CLATTER! KLANK!

WHAT MANNER OF CREATURE IS THIS?

A STRANGE-LOOKING URCHIN!

METHINKS HE IS A FOREIGNER! CANS'T THOU SPEAK?

SURE! I'M A NEW MAN IN YER GANG!

A NEW MAN? HAW! HAW!

I SAY A MERE INFANT!

IF YOU ARE A MAN, LITTLE ONE, I WOULD FAIN TEST THY STRENGTH! SMITE ME ON THE JOWLS!

WELL—IF THAT'S TH' WAY YA WANT T' PLAY—O.K.—I'LL DO IT!

SMACK!

SO! AND NOW IT IS MY TURN!

NAY! THOU ASKED FOR IT, METHINKS!

LET TH' BIG PALOOKA COME! I CAN TAKE CARE OF HIM!

VERY WELL! SO BE IT! YOU SHALL FIGHT WITH LONG STAVES! MICKEY MOUSE AND LITTLE JOHN!

LITTLE JOHN! OH GOSH!

WALT DISNEY 6-28
© 1936, by Walt Disney Enterprises, World rights reserved.

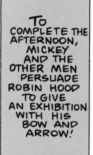

THOUGH I'D RATHER YA JUST GAVE YER MONEY WITHOUT FIGHTING!

OH, THAT'S ALL RIGHT! I ENJOY FIGHTING!

OKAY! I GUESS I'LL JUST HAFTA GO THROUGH WITH IT T' GET YER MONEY!

HERE GOES!

CRACK! WHOP! POPPETY POP!

DO YA GIVE UP YET?

POP WHAOK! SOCK!

METHINKS THAT ROBIN HOOD MUST BE VERY PROUD, INDEED, TO HAVE SO VALIENT A FIGHTER IN HIS BAND!

SO! SMARTIN' OFF WITH ME, EH? WELL—LET'S SEE YA STOP **THIS** ONE!

THIS REMINDS ME OF ONCE WHEN I FOUGHT LITTLE JOHN! ASK HIM ABOUT HIS SCARS!

CRACK!

WOP!

INCREDIBLE! THIS IS THE FIRST TIME SOMEONE GOT ME OFF MY FEET!

GOSH! DID I HURT YA?

NOT MUCH! BUT NEVER BEFORE HAVE I RECEIVED AN **UPPERCUT** FROM A **DOWNWARD** BLOW!

HERE, MY LAD! THOU HAST EARNED THE MONEY!

THOU HAST ROBBED ME FAIRLY AND SQUARELY!

OH GOSH! I DON'T NEED THAT MUCH MONEY!

YA SEE, I'M NOT REALLY A ROBBER AT ALL! SO ALL I WANT IS ENOUGH T' MAKE ROBIN HOOD **THINK** THAT I AM!

VERY WELL! WE SHALL DIVIDE THE MONEY! EACH WILL TAKE HALF!

ARE YA SURE? I WANTA BE FAIR, YA KNOW!

TAKE IT—AND WELCOME! AND TO PROVE MY GOOD WILL I SHALL GIVE THEE A NOTE TO BE DELIVERED TO ROBIN HOOD!

THERE! TAKE THIS TO THY MASTER! HE IS—A FRIEND OF MINE!

GEE! THANKS! THAT'S SURE GOOD OF YA!

WELL, SO LONG! IT WAS REAL NICE FIGHTIN' WITH YOU!

THE PLEASURE HATH BEEN ALL MINE! FAREWELL, MY FRIEND!

I DON'T KNOW WHO THAT GUY IS, BUT HE'S SURE A SWELL EGG! MAYBE I SHOULD'VE ASKED 'IM IF HE WANTED T' JOIN TH' GANG!

HERE YA ARE, ROBIN HOOD! NOT BAD FOR TH' FIRST TIME EH?

BY MY TROTH! 'TIS GOLD! WHOM DID YOU ROB, MY FRIEND? SOME RICH, FAT MERCHANT?

NO SIR! I GOT IT FROM A **KNIGHT**! I FOUGHT HIM AN' HE HANDED IT OVER! WHAT'S MORE, HERE'S A LETTER T' PROVE IT! HE SAYS HE KNOWS YA!

LISTEN TO THIS LETTER!

WELL?

"THIS MAN DEFEATED ME IN FAIR COMBAT! HE IS A GALLANT FIGHTER AND A CREDIT TO YOUR BAND! BUT I COMMAND THAT NEVER AGAIN SHALL HE BE SENT TO ROB WAYFARERS!"

COMMANDS? WHO IS HE?

RICHARD, THE LION-HEARTED! KING OF ALL BRITAIN!

8-9

164

HOW DOST THOU ENJOY LIFE IN SHERWOOD FOREST?

PRETTY WELL! ONLY I THOUGHT THERE'D BE MORE ADVENTURES AN' EXCITEMENT AN' STUFF!

ADVENTURES! UPON MY SOUL, IS NOT DOING BATTLE WITH KING RICHARD EXCITING ENOUGH?

OH YEAH, SURE! BUT I THOUGHT YA FOUGHT DRAGONS, AND RESCUED MAIDENS AN' SUCH!

I FEAR ALL THE DRAGONS ARE GONE! 'TIS A PITY! ST. GEORGE SLEW THE LAST ONE!

THEN HOW ABOUT A MAIDEN IN DISTRESS? AREN'T THERE ANY AROUND?

OH YES! PLENTY! WHY THERE IS HARDLY A CASTLE IN THE COUNTRY THAT DOESN'T HOLD AT LEAST ONE!

WELL, FER GOSH SAKES! WHY NOT RESCUE SOME OF 'EM?

NOT ME! BUT YOU CAN, IF YOU LIKE!

DO YOU KNOW OF SOME BEAUTIFUL MAIDEN IN DISTRESS?

BEAUTIFUL? THAT'S PRETTY DIFFICULT!

HOW ABOUT MAID MINERVA? I HEARD LAST WEEK THAT SHE IS BEING HELD IN DURANCE VILE!

WHERE?

FOLLOW ME, MY LAD! BUT I WARN YOU—THIS IS PROBABLY THE MOST DANGEROUS SPORT IN ALL MERRIE ENGLAND!

'TIS NOT FAR NOW! AND THEN—I WILL LEAVE THEE! AT THE CASTLE, THOU MUST GO IT ALONE!

MAID MINERVA IS WAITING IN THAT TOP ROOM! NOW—ALL YOU ARE GOING TO HAVE TO DO IS BRING HER DOWN!

FER GOSH SAKES!

8-16

Walt Disney

MICKEY BRAZENLY GOES TO THE FRONT DOOR OF THE CASTLE IN ORDER TO RESCUE THE BEAUTIFUL MINERVA!

DEFEND YOUR-SELVES!

WHY SHOULD WE? ARE WE BEING ATTACKED?

I'VE COME HERE TO RESCUE A MAIDEN IN DISTRESS!

OH! WHY DIDN'T YOU SAY SO? I WAS WORRIED THERE FOR A MINUTE!

SIR BAFFLEBRANE WILL SHOW YOU TO HER ROOM! AND IF YOU WANT TO FIGHT ON THE WAY, JUST FOR FUN, HERE IS A SWORD!

YA MEAN YER NOT GONNA STOP ME?

WHY SHOULD WE? I'M SURE MAID MINERVA WOULD BE DELIGHT-ED!

IT IS THIS WAY, MY FRIEND!

I DON'T GET IT! ISN'T SHE IN DISTRESS?

SURE! BUT SHE WAS IN DISTRESS BEFORE SHE CAME HERE!

WHAT ABOUT ?

IT'S SIMPLE! SHE WANTS TO GET MARRIED! SO SHE CAME TO STAY IN DURANCE VILE UNTIL SOME SAP WOULD COME ALONG TO RESCUE HER!

Ye Maiden in Distress

WELL GO RIGHT IN!

HEY! WAIT A MINUTE! DO YA MEAN IF I RESCUE HER, SHE'LL WANT T' MARRY ME?

Ye Durance Vile

OF COURSE! YOU HAVE TO MARRY HER! IT'S THE CUSTOM!

TH' CUSTOM BE HANGED!

NOW I KNOW WHY ROBIN HOOD SAID THAT THIS RESCUIN' STUFF WAS SO DANGEROUS!

EITHER RESCUE HER OR ANSWER TO ME!

8-23

Walt Disney

166

WHAT A NICE COUPLE!

LISTEN! I'M NOT GONNA MARRY **ANYBODY**—AT LEAST FOR A THOUSAND YEARS! UNDERSTAND?

IT WILL BE EITHER A WEDDING—OR A **FUNERAL** FOR YOU! TAKE THY CHOICE!

UH—WELL—IF YOU PUT IT THAT WAY—

GOODNESS? ISN'T THIS ROMANTIC? A MILITARY WEDDING!

THAT'S SURE TH' **ONLY** WAY IT'S GONNA **BE** A WEDDING!

ART THOU A PRINCE? A DUKE? OR A KNIGHT? OR WHAT?

NONE OF 'EM! I JUST DECIDED I'M AN AWFUL **SUCKER**!

BUT MAYBE WHEN WE GET T' SHERWOOD FOREST—ROBIN HOOD'LL FIX IT FOR ME!

HO MICKEY! I SEE THOU HAST TAKEN THY BRIDE!

BUT, ROBIN—LISTEN! I TELL YA I—

HULLO! COME FORTH MY MERRY MEN! A WEDDING IS IN BLOOM!

GO AHEAD, FRIAR TUCK! LET THE CEREMONY PROCEED!

© 1936, by Walt Disney Enterprises, World rights reserved. 9-13

WALT DISNEY

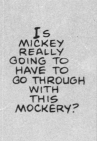

IS MICKEY REALLY GOING TO HAVE TO GO THROUGH WITH THIS MOCKERY?

WE HAVE GATHERED HERE TO WITNESS THE WEDDING OF SIR MICKEY MOUSE AND MAID MINERVA!

THAT'S WHAT **YOU** THINK!

AFTER ALL, YOU GUYS ARE NUTHIN' BUT A BUNCH OF ILLUSTRATIONS IN A CHEAP PICTURE BOOK!

MARRYIN' ONE OF YER DIZZY DAMES 'UD BE BAD ENOUGH—BUT T' MARRY A **PICTURE** OF ONE OF 'EM WOULD BE **AWFUL**! SO I WON'T DO IT—AN' THAT'S FINAL!

WHAT AN INSULT!

YOU VARLET!

LET'S DRAG HIM TO THE **STAKE** AND USE HIS COWARDLY HEART AS A TARGET!

THOU WILT PAY FOR THIS!

HEY WAIT!—WELL FER GOSH SAKES, KING RICHARD'S COMING!

BOW DOWN, THOU SCURVY KNAVES! BOW DOWN TO THY KING!

HOLD KNAVE! AND WHERE ART THOU GOING?

'TIS MICKEY MOUSE!

AFTER HIM!

HE'S INSULTED OUR KING!

© 1936, by Walt Disney Enterprises, World rights reserved. 9-20

WALT DISNEY

167

MICKEY MOUSE AND THE SEVEN GHOSTS

MICKEY MOUSE AND THE SEVEN GHOSTS

BUT, SERGEANT, I SAW ONE OF 'EM!

THAT'S FOOLISH, MY BOY! THERE **ARE** NO GHOSTS!

I TELL YA, I **SAW** IT WITH MY OWN EYES! LISTEN! WILL YA GO UP WITH ME—AN' SEE FOR YOURSELF?

NO! NO! NO! I ABSOLUTE-LY REFUSE! IT'S SILLY! I WAS UP THERE ONLY LAST NIGHT AND I WON'T GO BACK! IT'S— IT'S—

HEY, SARGE!

HERE'S YER HAT AN' YER GUN THAT YUH DROPPED AN' A BILL FOR TH' WINDOW YUH BUSTED, JUMPIN OUT O' TH' COLONEL'S HOUSE LAST NIGHT!

I TELL YA, SOMEBODY'S GOT T' DO SOMETHIN' ABOUT THOSE GHOSTS UP AT TH' COLONEL'S!

YEAH, MICKEY! I GUESS SO!

YOU AN' I ARE GONNA FIND OUT WHO THEY ARE AN' WHY THEY'RE HANGIN' AROUND!

ARE WE? HOW?

WE'LL START A DETECTIVE AGENCY AN' THEN WE CAN INVESTIGATE TH' CASE!

SHUCKS MICKEY— WHY NOT JUST ASK TH' GHOSTS?

I'VE GOT A HUNCH THERE'S MORE TO THIS THAN ANY-BODY THINKS! AN' IT'S GONNA TAKE SOME REAL DETECTIVE WORK T' GET T' TH' BOTTOM OF IT!

HI, FELLERS! OPENIN' A NEW STORE?

A DETECTIVE AGENCY! YOU COULD BE IN IT, IF YOU'RE NOT TOO SCARED!

WHO? ME? **SCARED?** I'LL FIGHT BOTH O' YA! I'LL FIGHT ANY FIVE GUYS IN TOWN!

WELL—OKAY! WE NEED TH' HELP, BUT YA GOTTA PROMISE NOT T' BACK OUT!

SURE! WHAT ARE YA GONNA DETECT— ROBBERS?

NOPE! WE'RE GOING UP TO COLONEL BASSETT'S AN' CLEAN OUT THAT NEST O' GHOSTS!

ACME DETECTIVE AGENCY
SLEUTHING-SHADOWING and GHOST EXTERMINATING

R R RING

WE JUST GOTTA WAIT FOR COLONEL BAS-SETT T' PHONE!

MEBBE THAT'S HIM!

HELLO! IS THIS THE ACME DETECTIVE AGENCY?

YES, SIR! PRESIDENT MOUSE SPEAKING!

YES, SIR! THAT'S WHY WE'RE HERE! AN' WHAT'S MORE, WE—

YOU'RE GONNA GET RID OF TH' GHOSTS, EH?

HOOHOOHOOHOHOHAHAHH

CLICK!

HELLO! COLONEL BASSETT? THIS IS THE ACME DETEC-TIVE AGENCY! WE'D LIKE TH' JOB OF EXTERMIN-ATING YOUR GHOSTS!

TH' PRESIDENT— THAT'S ME—HAS WORKED FOR TH' SECRET SERVICE AN' ONE OF MY ASSISTANTS KNOWS TH' GHOSTS PERSONALLY!

MY OTHER ASSIS-TANT IS AWFUL BRAVE—AN' OUR PRICES ARE REASONABLE! IF YOU'LL DROP IN SOMETIME—

PARDON ME, SIR! A CUSTOMER JUST CAME IN!

YOU'RE HIRED!

HIRED FOR **WHAT**?

TO GET RID OF THE GHOSTS! I'M COLONEL BASSETT!

SIT DOWN, COLONEL! TELL ME EVERY THING YA KNOW ABOUT TH' GHOSTS!

THE FIRST ONE WAS UNCLE AB-NER, WHO DIED TEN YEARS AGO! WE HAD A LOT OF FUN TALKING ABOUT OLD TIMES!

YA MEAN—YA SAT AROUND—AN' **CHATTED** WITH 'IM?

YES! IT WAS A BIG MISTAKE! HE LIKED IT SO MUCH HE BROUGHT ALL HIS FRIENDS!

UNDERSTAND—I DON'T MIND THEM HAVING A LITTLE FUN, BUT THE SEVEN OF THEM THROW WILD PARTIES EVERY NIGHT—

AND IT MAKES IT ENTIRELY TOO HARD TO KEEP SERVANTS!

AT FIRST I THOUGHT THEY WERE ALL ANCESTORS—I TRIED TO MAKE THEM COMFORTABLE! I CONSIDERED IT MY DUTY AS A HOST!

EVEN WHEN THEY DROVE MY WIFE AND SERVANTS SCREAMING FROM THE HOUSE, I WAS GRACIOUS TO THEM!

AND THEN, SUH, CAME THE **HORRIBLE, TERRIBLE** REALIZATION!

GOSH! WHAT HAPPENED?

I REALIZED, SUH, THAT I HAVE BEEN ENTERTAINING GHOSTS THAT ARE NOT THE GHOSTS OF GENTLEMEN!

THEN WHAT DID YOU DO, COLONEL BASSETT?

WHAT **COULD** I DO, SUH! I ORDERED THEM TO **LEAVE**!

AND WHAT DID THEY SAY TO THAT?

THEY REFUSED, SUH—LIKE THE CADS THEY ARE!

I AM A PATIENT MAN, SUH—BUT THEY HAVE ABUSED MY HOSPITALITY—AND I NO LONGER CONSIDER THEM MY GUESTS!

WHAT ARE YA GONNA DO NOW?

I'M GONNA KICK THE BLINKETTY-BLANKETTY SO-AN'-SOS **OUT**!

I HAVE KEPT CONTROL OF MYSELF AS LONG AS I COULD!

BUT THOSE GHOSTS THREATENED MY LIFE AND ABUSED MY HOSPITALITY—

AND NOW I'M **MAD**!!

WHAM

DO YOU BLAME ME, SIR?

AND IF YOU GET RID OF THOSE SEVEN GHOSTS, I WILL PAY YOU $5000!

OKAY, COLONEL! WE'LL BE AT YOUR HOUSE AS SOON AS WE GET OUR STUFF TOGETHER!

QUICK CHANGE ROOM

DISGUISES

LEMME SEE! WE'LL NEED A GUN, FINGERPRINT EQUIPMENT—

WELL—I'M READY! LET'S GO!

GOOD EVENING, GENTLEMEN! I WILL TELL THE MAWSTER YOU ARE HERE!

HEY! I THOUGHT YOU WERE COLONEL BASSETT!

I AM SUH! BUT WHEN THE GHOSTS CAME, ALL MY SERVANTS LEFT! WHAT COULD I DO?

IT IS ABSOLUTELY IMPOSSIBLE FOR A GENTLEMAN TO KEEP HOUSE WITHOUT SERVANTS! THEREFORE—

YOUR HATS AND COATS, PLEASE!

I THANK YOU, SUH!

YOUR GUN AND FLASH LIGHT, PLEASE!

TH' COLONEL SURE MAKES A SNOOTY BUTLER! PURTY TOUGH ON 'IM, THOUGH, WITH NO SERVANTS!

GOOD GOSH! NO SERVANTS!

THEN—**WHO** TOOK MY GUN AN' FLASHLIGHT?

I'LL BE DURNED! THIS HOUSE MUST BE HAUNTED!

174

THIS MIGHT BE SOMETHING, MICKEY! I'VE NOTICED THAT WHEN THE GHOSTS ARE IN THE ROOM, THERE'S A COLD WIND BLOWING!

I'VE SEEN YUH SHIVERIN', BUT I DIDN'T KNOW IT WAS A BREEZE!

PIPE DOWN, GOOFY! WE CAN'T MISS ANY BETS! I'LL—

DOGGONE TH' LUCK! THERE GO TH' LIGHTS AGAIN!

HEY! MICKEY! I TOLD YOU SO! FEEL THAT WIND?

BY GOLLY, DONALD! YOU'RE RIGHT! IT'S LIKE A COLD DRAFT! AN'—AN' EVERY WINDOW IN TH' ROOM IS CLOSED!

I'LL BE DURNED!

I'LL FIND THAT WIND, MICKEY! I'LL WET MY FINGER LIKE AN INDIAN—AN' I CAN TELL WHAT DIRECTION IT'S COMIN' FROM!

OKAY DONALD! THAT SHOULD WORK!

SLUPP! SLUPP! SLUPP!

ARE YA GETTIN' ANYWHERE? DOES IT WORK?

YOU BET! I'M GAININ' ON IT! IT'S GOOD AN' STRONG OVER HERE! BOY! I MUST BE GETTIN' AWFUL CLOSE TO—

QUA-A-A-ACK! QUACK-WACK WACK WACK WACK!

OWOOO!

WIIIRRRR-RACK CLATTER

HOOHOOHOHOHOHAHAHA!

QUA-ACK! WACK! WACK! WACK! WACK!

WHIRRRRR!

BUT IT WASN'T THERE WHEN TH' LIGHTS WENT OFF! WHADDAYUH MAKE OF IT?

PLENTY!

THERE ARE SOME SECRET PANELS IN HERE—'CAUSE THAT FAN'S NOT A GHOST—AN' IT COULDN'T GET THROUGH WALLS!

ALSO TH' GHOSTS OVERHEAR EVERYTHING WE SAY—OR THEY WOULDN'T HAVE KNOWN T' BRING IT HERE!

AN' SOMETHING IN THIS HOUSE MAKES A COLD WIND—AN' TH' GHOSTS DON'T WANT US T' KNOW ABOUT IT!

WHAT MAKES YUH THINK SO?

THERE MUST BE—OR THEY WOULDN'T HAVE TRIED T' PUT US OFF TH' TRACK WITH THAT FAN!

I'VE GOT A HUNCH COLONEL BASSETT KNOWS MORE ABOUT THESE GHOSTS THAN HE LETS ON! I'M GONNA SEE!

IF YOU'RE HUMAN, COME RIGHT IN! AND IF YOU'RE A GHOST, COME RIGHT THROUGH, SUH!

DON'T WORRY, SUH! MY INTENTION IS NOT TO HIT YOU OR ANYTHING!

ARE YA GONNA SOCK TH' GHOSTS, OR WHAT?

OH NO, SUH! NOTHING LIKE THAT! BUT WHEN I GET NERVOUS LIKE THIS, I ALWAYS BITE MY NAILS! AND IT'S MAKING MY NAILS VERY UNSIGHTLY, SUH!

HAVE YA EVER SEEN ALL SEVEN GHOSTS AT ONCE?

OH YES, SUH! QUITE OFTEN! TH' LAST TIME THEY THREATENED MY LIFE!

THEY DID? WHY DIDN'T YA TELL ME?

THEY WERE SO RUDE AND UNGENTLEMANLY THAT I WANTED TO FORGET ALL ABOUT IT!

WHAT HAPPENED, COLONEL? WHY DID THEY THREATEN YOU?

I WAS GOING UP TO THE ATTIC! THEY SAID IF I DID, I'D NEVER COME DOWN ALIVE!

WHAT DID YA DO?

WHAT ANY GENTLEMAN WOULD DO, SUH! I SIMPLY IGNORED THEM—AND I-UH-STAYED OUT OF THE ATTIC!

BY GOLLY! THAT'S TH' BEST NEWS I'VE HEARD TONIGHT!

SOMEHOW, IT DIDN'T IMPRESS ME THAT WAY, SUH!

I'M GOIN' T' HAVE A PEEK AT THAT ATTIC IF IT'S THE LAST THING I EVER DO!

BUT FIRST I'M GONNA FIND OUT WHETHER THESE GHOSTS ARE HUMAN—OR WHETHER THEY'RE REAL GHOSTS!

FIRST, COULD YOU HELP ME WITH THESE BUTTONS?

SURE, COLONEL! IT LOOKS LIKE YOUR FINGERS ARE ALL THUMBS!

WELL, FER GOSH SAKES!

MICKEY HAS FALLEN RIGHT THROUGH THE GROUND INTO AN UNDERGROUND TUNNEL THAT SEEMS TO BE FILLED WITH GUNS AND AMMUNITION!

WELL, BEFORE I START INVESTIGATIN' I'D BETTER TAKE A COUPLE OF THESE!

TEAR GAS BOMBS

I BET THAT DOOR LEADS TO THE BASEMENT! BUT WHERE'S TH' OTHER END OF THE TUNNEL?

GRENADES

HOT DIGGETTY! A LIGHT! THAT MUST BE TH' ENTRANCE!

SO THE TUNNEL LEADS ALL THE WAY TO THE OCEAN! BUT WHAT IS IT THERE FOR?

FOR TH' LOVE O' MIKE! A ROWBOAT! AN' IT'S HEADIN' RIGHT THIS WAY!

IT MUST BE FROM TH' SHIP OUT THERE THAT ANSWERED MY SIGNAL FROM TH' TRAFFIC GUN!

SURE! WHEN I FLASHED TH' GREEN LIGHT, THEY THOUGHT I WAS GIVIN' 'EM A SIGNAL T' COME AHEAD!

AN' I DON'T KNOW WHAT T' DO ABOUT IT—BUT WHATEVER IT IS—I'VE GOT TO DO IT FAST!

IT'S A CINCH TH' BOAT HAS SOMETHIN' T' DO WITH TH' GHOSTS! BUT WHAT! AN' WHY!

AN' WHAT ARE ALL THOSE GUNS FOR? I BETTER LOOK AROUND THIS TUNNEL AGAIN FOR A CLUE!

NOW—THAT DOOR LEADS TO TH' BASEMENT! BUT WHERE DOES THIS ONE GO?

GOSH! WILL YA LOOK AT THAT!

LEMME SEE! A SIGNAL IN TH' ATTIC, A TUNNEL LEADIN' TO TH' SEA, A WAREHOUSE, AN'—AN'—

WHOOPEE! I'VE GOT IT! THESE GUYS ARE SMUGGLERS!

HOW ABOUT DOIN' SOME TRICKS FOR US HUH'?

AND IN THE LIVING ROOM...

WHADDAYA WANT T' SEE?

YEAH! I'D L-L-LIKE TO SEE YOU D-D-DISAPPEAR!

AND MICKEY, MEANWHILE, CONTINUES TO EXPLORE THE SMUGGLERS' STORAGE ROOM!

BOY! LOOK AT TH' FOOD! THEY COULD HIDE HERE FOR A MONTH!

SUGAR

SUG

CORN POTATOES FLOUR

BY GOLLY! I KNEW THERE WAS SOMETHING PHONY ABOUT THOSE WALLS!

ENTRANCE TO SECRET PANELS

182

183

GOOD WORK, SERGEANT! I'M GLAD YA GOT MY PHONE CALL!

YEP! IT SURE WAS SMART OF ME TO FIGURE OUT YOUR TAPPING CODE!

WELL, LET'S JUST KEEP ON BEIN' SMART— AN' GET THIS GANG IN JAIL BEFORE SOMEBODY ELSE POPS IN ON US!

OKAY! TH' WAGON'S OUTSIDE WAITIN' FOR 'EM!

LEAVE TH' LEADER OF TH' GHOSTS! I'VE GOT A FEW QUESTIONS I WANT TO ASK HIM!

THERE ARE A FEW THINGS THAT NEED CLEARING UP!

I'LL QUESTION 'IM! I KNOW HIS KIND!

SO YOU WON'T TALK, EH? WELL— DO YOU KNOW WHO I AM?

YEAH! SURE I DO!

YOU'RE THE COP WHO JUMPED OUT OF THE WINDOW THE FIRST TIME YOU SAW US GHOSTS!

THIS IS YOUR LAST CHANCE! ARE YA GONNA TALK OR NOT?

SERGEANT! MAYBE YA BETTER LET ME ASK TH' QUESTIONS!

WHAT STARTED ALL THIS IN THE FIRST PLACE?

WE WANTED THIS HOUSE, SEE?

YEAH! GO AHEAD—

IT'S A PERFECT SPOT! SO WHEN TH' COLONEL WOULDN'T SELL, WE THOUGHT WE'D SCARE HIM OUT!

WE NEVER THOUGHT WE'D BUCK UP AGAINST ANY-BODY WITH BRAINS!

OH YEAH?

WE THOUGHT WE'D BE DEALING WITH YOU!

TELL ME HOW I COULD'VE SHOT THROUGH YA WITHOUT HURTIN' YA!

YOU DIDN'T! THE FIRST SHOT WAS A BLANK!

I THOUGHT OF THAT! BUT THE SECOND TIME I LOADED IT MYSELF!

AND YOU NEARLY PLUGGED SPIKE, TOO!

BUT AS SOON AS HE SAW THE GUN, HE DISAPPEARED AND JUMPED SIDE-WAYS!

YOU JUST SHOT WHERE HE HAD BEEN!

OF COURSE! THAT EXPLAINS EVERYTHING!

AND I THOUGHT HE WAS ONE OF MY ANCESTORS! TSK! TSK!

AN' HOW DID YOU APPEAR AN' DISAP-PEAR WHEN YA WANTED TO?

TURN OFF TH' LIGHTS AN' I'LL SHOW YOU!

WE'RE COATED WITH PHOSPHORESCENT PAINT— SO WE SHINE IN THE DARK! WHEN WE WANT TO DISAPPEAR WE PULL CLOAKS OVER US—

—LIKE THIS, SEE?

THAT'S TH' SLICKEST IDEA I EVER SAW!

OKAY, SERGEANT! TURN ON TH' LIGHTS!

WELL, FER— HE'S GONE!

IT APPEARS THAT THE GHOST HAS PULLED ONE FINAL DISAPPEAR-ING ACT!

HE'S TRICKED US!

GAWSH! MEBBE HE IS A GHOST!

184

MEBBE YUH BETTER TAKE KEER OF IT FUR ME! I'VE GOT A HOLE IN MY POCKET!

THEN PUT IT IN A SOCK TILL YA BUY A NEW SUIT!

THAT WOULDN'T DO NO GOOD! THERE'S HOLES IN MY SOCKS, TOO!

WHAT ARE YA GONNA DO WITH YOUR SHARE, DONALD?

I'M GONNA SPEND THE WHOLE THING! OBOY! AM I GONNA HAVE FUN!

I'LL BUY A NEW CAR—AND CLOTHES—AND A HOUSE—AND A BOAT—AND TAKE A LONG TRIP—AND—

HOW BIG DO YOU THINK THAT CHECK IS?

BIG ENOUGH! MY SHARE'S NEARLY $1700, AIN'T THAT RIGHT?

YEAH! BUT DONALD—

AND THEN I'LL INVEST THE REST AND LIVE OFF THE INTEREST!

!

DECIDING THAT IT IS USELESS TO TALK SENSE TO DONALD, MICKEY HANDS HIM HIS SHARE OF THE REWARD! AND GIVES OUT SOME MONEY TO GOOFY AS WELL!

I'LL TAKE CARE OF YOUR REWARD, GOOFY BUT YA OUGHTA SPEND PART OF IT YOURSELF!

WELL, OKAY, MICKEY

HERE'S FIFTY BUCKS! IT'S ALL YOURS!

YUH MEAN— I CAN JUST GO OUT AN' BUY SOMETHIN'! GAWSH!

GOOD OLD GOOFY! I'LL BET THAT'S MORE MONEY THAN HE'S EVER HAD IN HIS LIFE!

TWO HOURS LATER— MICKEY GOES TO ANSWER HIS DOORBELL!

WELL—HOW DO I LOOK?

WHAT'S TH' MATTER, GOOFY? ARE YA SICK?

NOPE! I'M A-THINKIN' BEAUTIFUL THOUGHTS!

WELL, FER— WHAT BROUGHT THIS ON?

BEAUTIFUL THINGS ALLUS MAKES ME FEEL SORTA SAD-LIKE!

AN' WHEN I LOOK AT MYSELF IN TH' MIRROR IN MY NEW SUIT—

AN' I SEE HOW PURTY I LOOK, IT JEST MAKES ME FEEL LIKE CRYIN'!

GOOFY! WHERE'S YOUR NEW SUIT? MICKEY TOLD ME HOW BEAUTIFUL IT WAS!

YEAH! IT'S AWFUL PURTY!

BUT THE NEXT DAY GOOFY IS WEARING HIS OLD CLOTHES AGAIN!

THEN WHY NOT WEAR IT?

WELL— I WASN'T GONNA TELL NOBODY— BUT—WELL—SHUCKS —I GUESS IT WON'T HURT NONE!

YUH SEE— I NEVER MENTIONED IT, BUT FUR A LONG TIME I BEEN HOPIN' THET SOME DAY TH' RIGHT GAL 'UD COME ALONG!

AN' IF SHE DID, I—HUH—I—I WANTED TUH SAVE IT FUR MUH WEDDIN'!

THE END

186

MICKEY MOUSE ON SKY ISLAND

MICKEY MOUSE ON SKY ISLAND

WITH TWO SETS OF CONTROLS IN THEIR PLANE, MICKEY BEGINS GOOFY'S FIRST FLYING LESSON!

THAT STICK IS TH' CONTROL LEVER! TO GO HIGHER, YA PULL IT BACK, AN'—

YUH MEAN—LIKE THIS?

HEY! FER GOSH SAKES! LEGGO OF TH' STICK! WE GOTTA TURN BACK OVER!

LEGGO? DO YUH WANT ME TUH GET HURT?

GOLLY! I GOTTA DISENGAGE TH' REAR CONTROLS AN' GO INTO A BARREL ROLL!

HERE WE GO! HANG ON, GOOFY!

THAT'S WHUT I'M DOIN'!

WHEWWWWW!

YUH KNOW—UNLESS A GUY WAS PURTY KEERFUL LIKE I AM, FLYIN' MIGHT BE KIND O' DANGEROUS!

HOW'D YA HAPPEN T' FALL OUT OF TH' PLANE, GOOFY?

I DIDN'T MEAN TO!

ALL OF A SUDDEN TH' PLANE WAS UPSIDE DOWN—AN' I WASN'T 'N IT!

WHY DIDN'T YA HAVE YER BELT FASTENED, YA BIG DUMMY?

SHUCKS! I WASN'T WORRYIN' ABOUT A BELT!

WHY—THESE CLOTHES DON'T EVEN NEED SUSPENDERS!

MICKEY DECIDES THAT GOOFY'S FIRST FLYING LESSON HAS ENDED FOR THE DAY!

WOT YUH GOT THAR, MICKEY?

IT'S A SPECIAL AVIATION CAMERA!

WHUT DO YUH DO-TAKE PITCHERS OF AVIATORS?

NO, YA TAKE PICTURES FROM AIRPLANES!

SURE! YA PUSH THIS LITTLE GADGET—AN' TAKE TH' CAMERA TO A DRUGSTORE—

DO YA KNOW ANYTHING ABOUT CAMERAS GOOFY?

CLICK!!

AN' TH' NEXT DAY YUH GOT A PITCHER! IT'S EASY!

GOOFY! WHY DON'T YA GET A PICTURE OF THAT MOUNTAIN? WHEN I BANK YOU SHOOT IT!

THAT SEEMS SIMPLE ENOUGH, BUT—

GAWSH! WHEN YUH TIPPED TH' PLANE, I DROPPED TH' CAMERA OVERBOARD!

BUT DON'T WORRY! I'LL GIT TH' PITCHER WITH MY OWN CAMERA!

PLOP!

OH, GOOFY, YA BIG DUMMY! HOW COULD YOU HAVE DROPPED OUR CAMERA OVERBOARD?

HEY, MICKEY! DO YUH KNOW THAT GUY WAVIN' AT US?

LOOK AT THAT!

YEAH! I SEE HIM!

OMIGOSH! DO YUH SEE THAT, MICKEY! HE'S—HE'S—

FUR GAWSH SAKES! HE'S RIDIN' IN AN AUTO!

190

SINCE IT IS A PERFECTLY CLEAR SUNNY DAY, MICKEY DECIDES THE BLACK CLOUD IS WORTH INVESTIGATING!

AN', GOOFY, IT'S SUCH A FUNNY SHAPE!

WELL, FER— HEY! LOOK!

GAWSH, MICKEY! THEM'S ROOTS!

ROOTS GROWIN' IN TH' SKY? AM I GOIN' CRAZY?

MEBBE WE FLEW CLEAR AROUND TH' WORLD!

WELL—GOOFY! WE'RE GONNA FIND OUT!

I DON'T BELIEVE IT! IT'S IMPOSSIBLE!

ME NEITHER! LET'S GO HOME AN' FERGIT TH' WHOLE THING!

WELL, NOW THAT YOU'VE FOUND ME COME ON DOWN!

IT'S—IT'S HIM!

LISTEN, MICKEY! I GOT A LOT O' WORK T' DO AT HOME, AN'—

NOT A CHANCE, GOOFY!

WHERE SHOULD WE LAND?

JOOST A MINUTE! I FIX!

HEY! WHAT TH'—

DON'T WORRY, MINE FRIEND! YOUR PLANE IS SAFE! COME RIGHT DOWN!

IT'S OKAY! JOOST STEP DOWN!

DO YA HAVE A LADDER?

YOU DON'T NEED A LADDER! JOOST WALK DOWN!

DO YA MEAN WE SHOULD JUMP?!

NO, MINE FRIEND! JOOST STEP OVER AND DOWN YOU COME!

THAT'S WHAT I'M SKEERED OF!

WELL, FER GOSH SAKES! GOOFY! IT'S—IT'S LIKE WALKIN' DOWN STAIRS!

SO AT LAST MICKEY MEETS THE AMAZING SCIENTIST ON HIS STILL MORE AMAZING ISLAND IN THE SKY!

WELCOME! I AM DOCTOR EINMUG!

MY NAME IS MICKEY MOUSE-AN' THIS IS GOOFY!

YES, I SEE!

WILL YA TELL ME HOW YA DO ALL THIS STUFF, SIR? FLYIN' AUTOS-AN' KEEPIN' THIS PLACE IN TH' AIR-AN' EVERYTHING!

SURELY!

THERE IS ENOUGH POWER IN A GLASS OF WATER TO GET A SHIP ACROSS THE OCEAN-IF ALL THE POWER IS UTILIZED!

YES, BUT—

UNDERSTAND? WELL—I SIMPLY UTILIZE IT! THAT'S ALL!

SEE, MICKEY! I KNEW THERE WAS NUTHIN' TO IT!

CHEMICALS GO IN THAT FUNNEL-THROUGH THOSE TUBES—AND ARE CONVERTED—

—TO STEAM AT HIGH PRESSURE-CHARGED WITH MILLIONS OF VOLTS OF ELECTRICITY-IS SHOT THROUGH THOSE COILS AND TUBES—

194

MICKEY HERE SHOWED ME THAT CRIME DON'T PAY! SO I WON'T PESTER YUH ANYMORE, DOC!

FROM NOW ON, I'M JUST GONNA DO GOOD! I REALLY WANT TUH BE FRIENDS! WHADDAYUH SAY, MICKEY? WILL YUH LET ME?

C'MON, PETE! HAVE YOU REALLY REFORMED?

I SURE HAVE, MICKEY! AN' I'M A CHANGED MAN! AN' I SEEN TH' ERROR O' MUH WAYS!

PETE'S WHOLE STORY SEEMS A LITTLE **TOO GOOD** TO BE TRUE!

AN' I EVEN FORGIVE YUH FER ALL TH' MEAN THINGS YUH DONE TUH ME!

LET US GO TO MY PLACE, UND TOAST DER REFORMATION! I HAFF SOME CHAMPAGNE UND—

NIX, DOC! IT'LL BE GRAPE JUICE FER ME! WHEN I REFORMS, I REFORMS CLEAN THROUGH!

COME RIGHT IN!

NICE PLACE, DOC! AN' I SURE FEEL SWELL BEIN' ON' TH' RIGHT SIDE O' TH' LAW!

HI, GOOFY, OL' PAL!

OH, HELLO!

GOOFY, DON'T YA REMEMBER PEGLEG PETE?

OH FUR GAWSH SAKES!

I DO!

LET US DRINK TO A BAD MAN GONE GOOD! CHAMPAGNE?

NO—GRAPE JUICE FOR ME!

YEAH! ME, TOO!

WELL—DOWN TH' HATCH, BOYS! AN' IF THIS DON'T PROVE I'VE REFORMED— NUTHIN' WILL!

IT'S SHORE FUNNY HOW HE'S CHANGED, AIN'T IT?

IT SURE IS!

MICKEY, OL' PAL—REMEMBER THAT TIME ON TH' SCHOONER WHEN I KICKED YUH AN' SLAPPED YUH ALL OVER TH' DECK? HAW! HAW!

YEAH! AN' THEN I GOT LOOSE AN' BEAT YA UP, AN' JAILED YA FOR SMUGGLIN'! I REMEMBER **THAT**, OL' PAL!

YEAH! I REMEMBER! WHAT'S MORE, I MADE UP MY MIND RIGHT THEN THAT—

OOP-AHUMPH-RUMPH-HOFF!

—I JUST GOT WHAT I DESERVED! GOSH! I WAS AWFUL BAD IN THEM DAYS!

DOCTOR, COULD ANYBODY ELSE LINE UP ATOMS IF THEY HAD YOUR FORMULA?

YES! **SOME** OTHER MEN COULD DO IT!

HEY, DOC! HUH—I'M JUST **CURIOUS** ABOUT WHERE YUH KEEP TH' FORMULA!

I WILL TELL YOU!

BUT YOU MUST KEEP IT A SECRET!

SURE, DOC! YUH KIN TRUST ME WITH **ANY**THING!

I KEEP IT WHERE NO ONE WILL EVER SEE IT—UNLESS SOMEDAY I DECIDE TO GIFF IT TO HIM!

WELL, MICKEY—ARE WE GONNA GO HOME TONIGHT?

196

YOU'LL NEVER GET THAT FORMULA AS LONG AS I'M ALIVE!

OH YEAH?

ANOTHER CRACK LIKE THAT OUT O' YUH AN' YUH WON'T **BE** ALIVE!

OW!

THAT'S A GAME CALLED "LOOP THUH SNOZZLE!"

SEVEN O'CLOCK! HMMM! IN TWO HOURS, TH' SAFE 'LL OPEN AN' I'LL BE ON MUH WAY WID DAT FORMULA!

I DON'T WANT YUH TUH MISS NUTHIN'— SO LET'S ALL GATHER AROUND THUH SAFE, CHUMMY-LIKE!

YOU GUYS IS LUCKY! IT AIN'T EVERYBODY WHO GITS RESERVED SEATS TO A BILLION-DOLLAR ROBBERY!

WHILE WE'RE WAITIN' FUR THUH SAFE TUH OPEN, LET'S DRINK A TOAST TO THUH ROBBERY!

IT LOOKS LIKE PEGLEG PETE IS GOING TO GET AWAY WITH THIS TERRIBLE CRIME! WHAT CAN STOP HIM NOW!?

TO THUH BIGGEST JOB EVER PULLED—AN' TO THUH GUY WHAT PULLED IT—

GENTLEMEN— THANK YOU FOR YOUR APPLAUSE!

AW, GOSH, DOC! YOU OUGHTA BE DRINKIN', TOO! AFTER ALL, IT'S YOUR CHAMPAGNE!

LAP IT UP, BOYS! THERE'S PLENTY MORE WHERE THIS CAME FROM!

I'M GONNA GO LOOK AROUND! MEBBE I KIN FIND SOMETHIN' **ELSE** I LIKE!

BUT DON'T WORRY! I'LL BE BACK IN PLENTY O' TIME—SO DON'T GO AWAY! HAW! HAW! GLUG! GLUG! GLUG! GLUG!

♪ OH, WHEN MUH SHIP COMES INTA PORT, YUH'LL FIND ME STANDIN' AT THUH WHEEL♪

GOSH, DOCTOR EINMUG! WHAT'RE WE GONNA DO? WE GOTTA STOP PETE!

DON'T WORRY! IT ISS ALREADY DONE!

IT IS NOT SURPRISING THAT THE DOCTOR HAS PROTECTED HIS FORMULA BUT HOW DID HE DO IT, TIED TO A CHAIR?

YA MEAN— HE WON'T GET IT?

DOT ISS RIGHT! YOU SEE MY MACHINERY MUST HAVE NEW CHEMICALS BY 8:30!

GEE! BUT WHAT'S GONNA HAPPEN IF IT DOESN'T GET 'EM BY THEN?

THE MACHINERY WILL STOP AND THIS WHOLE ESTATE WILL **CRASH** TO EARTH!

BUT DOCTOR EINMUG, WE'LL ALL BE DESTROYED!

DOT ISS RIGHT! BUT PEGLEG PETE SHALL NOT HAFF MINE FORMULA!

BUT ISN'T THERE SOMETHIN' YA COULD DO T' STOP IT?

NOT FROM HERE! I WOULD HAFF TO GET INTO MINE LABORATORY!

BUT WE'LL BE **KILLED!**

YAH! OF COURSE! BUT DER WRONG PERSONS WILL NEFFER GET HOLD OF DER FORMULA THIS WAY!

ISSN'T DOT A BEAUTIFUL WAY TO DIE?

BUT WHY JUST SIT HERE AN' WAIT— WHEN WE MIGHT BE ABLE T' DO SOMETHIN'!

YAH? WHAT?

TELL ME HOW T' PUT NEW CHEMICALS IN YOUR MACHINERY! IF I'M GONNA DIE, I MAY AS WELL DIE **TRYIN'!**

YAH! BUT YOU ARE TIED UP! HOW CAN YOU GET TO MINE LABORATORY?

BY BOUNCIN' ALONG ON THIS CHAIR LIKE PETE SHOWED ME!

WELL, MINE FRIEND! I COULD EASILY TELL YOU HOW TO PUT THE CHEMICALS IN MINE MACHINE, BUT I WON'T!

FOR GOSH SAKES! WHY NOT?

IF WE LIVE, PEGLEG PETE DOES ALSO! BUT I WILL LET YOU TRY ON ONE CONDITION!

SWELL! WHAT IS IT?

YOU MUST PROMISE NOT TO ADD THE CHEMICALS UNTIL YOU HAFF ABSOLUTELY SUBDUED PEGLEG PETE!

SO! YOU PULL LEVER "S" FORWARD, LEVER "K" BACKWARD, AN' OPEN VALVE "Q". IT ISS VERY SIMPLE!

SWELL! IS THAT ALL?

YAH! DOT ISS ALL! NOW DO YOU PROMISE TO SUBDUE PEGLEG PETE FIRST?

WELL – OKAY, DOCTOR! I PROMISE!

BECAUSE IF HE SHOULD GET MINE FORMULA, IT ISS BETTER WE SHOULD ALL DIE TOGETHER!

NOW I'VE GOTTA GO DOWNSTAIRS, LICK PETE, GET TO TH' LABORATORY, AN' HANDLE TH' LEVERS AN' VALVES – ALL BEFORE 8:30 – TIED T' THIS CHAIR!

AN' WILL YUH TRY T' FIND ME A SANDWICH, MICKEY?

WELL – IT'S A CINCH I CAN'T GET DOWNSTAIRS TIED UP LIKE THIS!

HOW WILL MICKEY GET TO THE LABORATORY AND TO PETE?

BY GOLLY! THERE'S A DOOR LEADING OUT ONTO TH' ROOF! MAYBE I CAN –

– GET OUT THIS WAY! GOSH! I WONDER WHERE PETE IS RIGHT NOW!

IT'S EIGHT O'CLOCK! IN JUST ONE HOUR, I'LL BE A BILLIONAIRE! PEGLEG PETE, THUH "ATOM KING"!

WELL – I KNOW I'LL BE KILLED IF I DON'T DO IT! AN' IF I DO TRY IT –

– I'LL PROBABLY STILL GET KILLED! IF I CAN ONLY LAND WITH TH' LEGS DOWN – I HAVE A CHANCE!

IF I DON'T – WELL, HERE GOES!

♪ OH, HAUL UP THUH ANCHOR AN' CAST OFF THUH LINES – ♪♪

DOGGONE TH' LUCK! HERE COMES PETE! NOW I CAN'T EVEN JUMP 'CAUSE HE'LL SEE ME! UNLESS –

BY GOLLY! IT'S ONE CHANCE IN A MILLION!

♪ MY SHIP IS A-SAILIN OUT TUH SEA! ♪

AN' SOON WE'LL BE BOUNDIN' OVER WAVES – YO HO! THAT'S THUH LIFE FUR ME!

BUT – HERE GOES!

ON A CLEAR, COLD ♪ NIGHT WHEN THUH MOON IS OUT O' SIGHT, AN' THUH WIND GOES A-WHISTLIN' THROUGH THUH SPARS – AN' ALL THAT WE CAN SEE IS – ♪

CRACK!

STARS!

BOY! WOT A KICK DAT CHAMPAGNE MUST O' HAD!

OHO! SO IT WAS YOU, HUH? WELL – I'LL LEARN YUH!

TAKE THAT, YUH LITTLE RAT!

GOOD GOSH!

HE'S GONNA FALL OFF!

HELP!

DON'T LET GO, MICKEY! I'LL BE GOOD—I PROMISE! I'LL NEVER HURT YOU NO MORE!

THERE YOU ARE!

MICKEY, I OWES MUH LIFE TUH YUH! AN' I ALLUS PAYS MUH DEBTS!

AN' THERE'S SUMPIN' ELSE I'VE OWED YUH—FER A LONG TIME!

AN' NOW'S THUH TIME TUH GIVE IT TUH YUH!

SMACK!

WHACK!

IT'S JEST LIKE YUH, YUH RAT—TUH SAVE MUH LIFE—

JEST SO'S I WON'T DO NUTHIN' TUH YUH!

WELL, IT WON'T WORK! SO LONG, MICKEY!

ZOOOM!

OH, IT'S TOO AWFUL! I CAN'T BEAR TO LOOK!

IF I WASN'T SO GLAD TUH BE RID O' HIM, I MIGHT ALMOST BE SORRY!

TAKE THAT, YA TUB O' LARD!

SMACK!

SO! YUH AIN'T DONE YET, HUH?

WELL—NOW I'M GONNA TAKE YUH APART!

I'VE GOT YUH NOW, YUH BLASTED LITTLE SWAB!

AN' I AIN'T GONNA LEGGO OF YUH TILL—

YEOW!

UNTIL I'M WHAT, PETE?

OOOOOF! OWW!

HELP! CUT IT OUT!